The Anti-Cyclops Papers
Volume One

Good Nazis In Office, Good Niggers In Jail

James Nathan Post

Writers Club Press
San Jose New York Lincoln Shanghai

Good Nazis In Office, Good Niggers In Jail

Writers Club Press
an imprint of iUniverse.com, Inc.

For information address:
iUniverse.com, Inc.
5220 S 16th, Ste. 200
Lincoln, NE 68512
www.iuniverse.com

ISBN: 0-595-19284-X

Printed in the United States of America

Dedication

This book is dedicated to:

Mark Steven Eisenberg and Shellee Renee,
editors of The Las Vegas Valley Explorer,
for publishing these viewpoints, and for helping to keep me focused
during times of frustration with the calling.

And to:

Dean Rosemary "Nurse Ratchet" Murphy
and
Principal Robert "Reverend Hale" Guery,

whose exemplary performances in the roles of
the tight-lipped grey-souled tough-love petty tyrant and
condescendingly sympathetic but willfully impotent bureaucrat
committed to protecting the illusions of the institutions they serve
at the expense of the individuals they claim to serve
motivated my first letter to The Valley Explorer,
which has led to the publishing of this book.

Cover painting by Famin d'Boy.

Contents

Crackpot Patriots

Are we really only crackpot idealists and intellectual Pollyannas who think the particulars of the Constitution are more than rhetorical statements used or denied at will by those who trade in power? Is belief in the truth of it like Santa Claus a pleasant myth we should acknowledge and grow past? At what point do I take in hand the trusting schoolboy I once was and admit that the world implied by the Bill Of Rights is not the real world at all. At what point do I concede that no Constitutional right exists to which agencies of the state are not granted enforceable exception by the courts? My copy of the Constitution weighs an ounce, in pamphlet form. Floors in the libraries are full of the arguments and rulings of various lawyers and judges proclaiming to "interpret" the precise meaning of its crudely unambiguous declarative statements. Those interpretations have largely supported granting the state exceptions to its Constitutional limits, and limiting the private citizen's Constitutional protections from state power. At what point do I concede there is no court in which the command structure—the state, the law, and the force—can be held accountable for exceeding Constitutional restraint?

There seems hardly any reason to encourage participation in the democratic process of election. The big-party faithful will toot their horns, cheer their slogans, and vote their party line. The internally-fuddled Reform Party will continue to get media coverage, because its lack of coherent ideology or definable agenda make it a scarecrow opponent. The freedomist's best kept secret, the Libertarian Party, will be denied exposure and ballot access because it does have coherent ideology and a definable agenda—precisely as represented by literal interpretation of the Bill Of Rights. Worse is recognition that no matter which party's champion gets into office, the offices will all be run exactly the same way, and the same laws will be enforced by the same agencies. It doesn't matter whether you choose Nikes or Adidas—you're gonna end up in a pair of rubber shoes, and you're gonna pay a hundred bucks for them. And you will learn to play ball, by the rules.

If we don't like it, what then, armed resistance? Even if armed like a fireteam of Marines, is it not beyond reality to imagine anyone might successfully resist enforcement of legislated rule? No matter what I think is meant by such phrases as, "....shall not be abridged," and "....shall make no law," there is in fact no power on earth to defend me from the full arsenal of armed enforcement of duly-enacted laws abridging each and every one of the rights in the Bill Of Rights. Where is the sense then in my whining that the Old Rules have been permanently broken by the lawmakers? At what point do I concede there nothing to be gained by it, and it might as well not be continued? And when that point is reached, what do I write in hope of encouraging those who would like to live as responsible free citizens in a world of personal rights and opportunities? The vote is a sham, the courts are a big-bucks crap shoot (or a rubber-stamp fine mill), and the number and power of agencies conducting surveillance and imposing control are increasingly increasing. To permit the state to protect us from pornography and political subversion, we surrendered market and media to control by monitoring and censorship. To permit the state to protect us from temptation to indulge ourselves with the Devil's marijuana, we surrendered absolute power to search and seize any person or property at will, and we built a huge system of courts and prisons. And now, as the "tune in—turn on" generation grows gray, those powers are turned upon another group of Americans—a group most surprised to find themselves suddenly confronted with the machine they eagerly authorized. If we thought the War On Drugs was a draconian violation of all sense of truth, logic, or righteousness, a destroyer of rights, a destroyer of lives, and destroyer of communities— well, hang on, because the War On Guns could make that look like a peaceful afternoon in the exercise yard. For his surly and disrespectful attitude to a mall guard, Metro Police recently held down and beat up a slender 18-year-old Boy I know, smacking his face into the street while taunting him, "Does that hurt, bitch? It's supposed to." They arrested him for "obstructing an officer." DEA guys wear sneakers, carry pistols, beat up, and arrest dangerous degenerate dope dealers who immorally pollute themselves and tempt children. The ATF are loyal and pious, self-sacrificing extreme-stress specialists who wear battle armor, carry Federally-authorized assault rifles, and shoot to kill subversive gun-cult terrorists who refuse to be lawfully disarmed. Patriots, I want you to know it really sucks, to say, "I told you so."

Addicted To The Hype

To save us from addicting ourselves, the drug-warmongers have placed us all in protective incarceration. So why do Americans seem to have no power to resist addiction? Because we are indoctrinated from childhood to justify it. "Gotta get it!" cheers the self-indulgent Granny, clutching her cola cans. "Having a Big Max attack?" the jock-idol tempts the Madonna clone drooling on his biceps. "Gotta cop my Pops," cracks the New Order Boy Scout as he suckers little brother out of the last lip-smacking pop. The lesson is clear: "Your desire is justification for getting it now, by any means, and you ought to desire it, because it is so good." That attitude—rationalized compulsive consumption for sensual gratification—is a good definition of addiction. It is the driving force behind the American economy, and the hallmark of the American way of life. It is glorified in every form, and our heroes are those with the biggest appetites. "Does this commercial give you tension headache? Buy prescription-strength Feelgoodol over the counter now!" Pharmaceutical corporations—the drug makers—produce an array of non-curative drugs intended only to make the patient feel good. Called sedatives, relaxants, tranquilizers, or anti-depressants, they are sold to produce essentially the same mild euphoric effect as marijuana. The millions of Americans "self-prescribing" marijuana are not treating terminal glaucoma, but choosing the herb because they get exactly what the drug sellers promise with their pills —relaxation and mood enhancement. Since that threatens the drugmakers' market strangle-hold, they insist marijuana has no medicinal validity and self-indulgent users immorally abuse themselves. "Potheads get high on the devil's weed; patients receive therapeutic amelioration from miracle drugs." Frankly, if I were dying of cancer, I might like marijuana for attitude adjustment, but give me real homegrown opium for pain. Yes, it is addictive, but so what? So is the patentable opium-derivative artificial-molecule junk the insurance companies which own the drug companies will pay the doctors to permit the pharmacists to sell.

Those who make the rules concerning which addictive or medicinal products are forbidden each have vested interests in other commodities. The principal illegal drugs have one thing in common: they may be obtained and used by the consumer without the intervention of financier, manufacturer, packager, advertiser, wholesaler, retailer, or government inspector, not to mention the IRS. Those who market synthetic drugs have proclaimed themselves authorities on the value of the natural ones, and the last word on why they must be forbidden. It is a protectionist assault on free trade, usurping the power of law enforcement to prevent people from using naturally available substances in competition with their market for prescribed synthetic drugs. Our government's brutal persecution of "self-abuse dissidents" is not war on drugs, nor even war on addiction, but simply a world war on disobedience, and the crime is not using drugs, but buying drugs from anyone but the government's dealers.

If we would make war on addiction, then instead of basing our lives on sensual consumption, we should learn to value a lifestyle of frugality, healthful moderation, and prudent restraint. Curiously, this attitude of delight in simple life is most clearly observable in the self-sufficient philosophy of the marijuana-using hippie subculture of the 1960's. Mainstream America declared that fondness for humble but euphoric peasant life to be "loss of social motivation" and still takes it as evidence of marijuana's harm. It is considered weakness of character to lack prideful ambition in America. Where personal success is measured in consumption power, and national success is measured in volume of trade, addiction is a principal measure of patriotism.

Marijuana doesn't promote a lifestyle of status consumption, which fact is held against it. But there is one drug that makes us obsessive and competitive, and makes us want sensual indulgence, and more, more, more. Cocaine is most attractive to the conditioned middle class precisely because it enhances those qualities of aggression, consumption, and ego-centrism our success-images glorify. The way to beat cocaine is certainly not by prohibition. That makes it the blue-chip high-octane fuel of the hottest high-risk, high-thrill guns-lawyers-and-big-bucks game around, exponentially multiplying its power to be used for evil or destructive (even if well-wishing) ends. Cocaine—like every other vice—is defeated only by learning that *all* compulsive consumption for sensual gratification is ultimately self-destructive and must be *voluntarily* overcome to survive. Unfortunately, this is a heretical notion in America, even if one to which almost everyone will lend lip service.

Drugs are not the cause of our country's problems, just another symptom of our decay into one more of the world's great cults of pride, greed, and power, consuming the biosphere from cloud-top to bedrock in our rush to build a higher pyramid, to be raised upon it, exalted by reverent multitudes, and rewarded with endless stimulation.

Who Needs Freedom?

A War on Drugs? Pray, who might be the enemy? The unemployable untouchables, the city sludge, are junkies, because the narcotic makes their unbearable world go away. The minimum-wage class are potheads, because the affordable euphoric makes their shabby lives bearably mellow. The labor class are into booze and bennies, one because it numbs their pain without suppressing their aggressiveness, and the other because it keeps them on the job. The yuppies, management, the power-seekers and ambitious—and the serious criminals—are on cocaine, because it keeps them tense and hungry, and it's where the money is. The Doc sells downers so Dad can get some sleep. Mom takes uppers to lose weight. Junior dreams of steroids so girls will think he's cute. Sis wants abortion pills 'cause some other boy was cute. A War on Drugs? In the words of the great political philosopher Pogo Possum, "We have met the enemy, and he is us."

The most severe tyranny is not of simple lust for power, but of those who are convinced controlling others' lives is their responsibility. The War On Drugs is a war by us on us, and its price is our freedom. It is the stupidest of all possible wars, because nobody wins. If the enforcers win, we are imprisoned. If the kingpins win, we are intoxicated. Those who believe the Constitution grants too much freedom, and who prefer unlimited government power may gain through its prosecution, but that is hardly to say anybody wins. It was the most basic premise of my political education that the greatest crime against mankind is the imposition of authoritarian socialist power regimes like those of Hitler and Stalin, and the medicine which cures such social disease is the freedom of informed citizens to act among themselves according to the Bill Of Rights. Hitler would take a second mortgage on his soul for the tools and powers granted to our Drug Czars.

It's my impression not many 21st Century Americans really desire or have any concept of day-to-day personal freedom. Most are happily locked into their worker/consumer slots enjoying the illusions which make up their perception of the world. It's hard to knock their lives. They are like the great ungulate herds that evolved to crop and fertilize the grasses of the plains, as they churn the beef, oil, and steel to grow fat and happy. Their existence certainly supports the case for socialism, and their willingness to join unions and sheep-cult religions shows they prefer things like that. P.T.Barnum said, "If He had not meant them to be shorn, God would not have made them sheep." These are good people, and they should have every right to be satisfied with their comfortable lives, notwithstanding they might look to some others like fat geldings locked to a treadmill in a padded stall with a virtual-reality hat over their heads. That's an important point: presuming one who would make of himself an activist for freedom is motivated by a desire to improve the general society, I'd say it's smart to avoid doing more damage to good people than what it is you're down on, like the Drug War does. And though the freedomist may champion freedoms that only the extremist will exercise, he must conduct himself in a manner which will protect the security of the working masses, no matter how numb from the neck up their keepers have them doped. It boils down to recognizing that to do something for "the people" of our country either as a system leader, or a revolutionary, our means and our ends must enable the best lives for the individuals which make up that illusory collective. Destroying a fat highly-ordered society in the name of granting to its members the freedom to behave otherwise than the order dictates is no better than destroying it to keep its members off marijuana. Given "freedom" to behave independently, what might cattle do? Wander from the herd? Stampede in all directions? Open a burger franchise? Or vote for a new bull and start butting heads picking a heifer to go make veal with? On the other hand, not all of us are beeves. The trick for those who would like to live by some other lifestyle, and must oppose the structure of the corral to do so, is to obtain the freedom to be different, without destroying the structure by which the ordered survive.

The means to obtain such voluntary cooperation of diverse individuals for a collective good is the full implementation of the Bill Of Rights, and the righteous protection of the citizen from violation of his rights by government or other citizens. To make such a society function, its people must be politically informed, respectfully tolerant of others as groups and individuals, and patriotically devoted to the government which protects their freedoms. Government should devote itself to defending and preserving the freedom of the people. Given such freedom, the people should devote themselves to the common good. That used to be called "The American Way."

Marijuana: Martyred In The Marketplace

Criminalization of hemp is an American tragedy with global and historic consequences. These facts are generally verifiable in the Encyclopedia Britannica, which was printed on Cannabis hemp paper for 150 years. Most high-quality books were hemp paper until the 1880's. It was legal to pay taxes with Cannabis hemp in America from 1631 until the early 1800's. George Washington and Thomas Jefferson grew it, and studied its many uses. Cannabis hemp is the longest, most durable, and longest-lasting natural fiber. From before Christ until the 1930's, 90% of all ships' sails were Cannabis hemp. The word 'canvas' is from Cannabis. 80% of all heavy textiles and rugs were hemp until the 1820's, when the industrial gin permitted cotton to be produced at lower cost. Even so, hemp was the second most widely used fiber until the 1930's, when it was renamed "marijuana" and outlawed as a "drug". Most of those fabrics have been replaced by synthetic fibers patented by DuPont and other petrochemical producers. Until 1937, most good paints were made with hemp seed oil, according to Sherwin Williams Paint Company speaking before Congress against the Hemp Tax Transfer Law. Over one hundred million pounds of hemp seed were consumed yearly for paint. After 1937, most paint used petrochemical oils made with DuPont patents. 90% of all paper was Cannabis hemp until 1883. The Gutenberg Bible in the 15th Century, Poor Richard's Almanac in the 18th, and Mark Twain in 19th were all printed on hemp linen paper. It is likely the Declaration of Independence is printed on hemp, though US Government Archives will not be more specific than "linen." Rembrandt and Van Gogh painted on hemp canvas. According to US Archives, hemp paper is most durable and long-lasting, the perfect archival medium.

In 1883, DuPont's patented woodpulp-sulfide process made it possible to produce cheap paper from evergreen trees and sulfuric acid, a petroleum bi-product. It decayed rapidly, but was useful for mass publication, like newspapers. In 1916, a process was patented to make inexpensive pulp hemp paper. Using modern technology, it could replace our present need for paper (except newsprint) with better paper, and it would eliminate the acid rain created by the sulfide process. Agriculture Department stated one acre of Cannabis hemp for paper pulp would replace four-and-one-half acres of evergreen trees. In the 1930's, technology to use the 1916 hemp patent became available. Hearst Paper Manufacturing Division stood to lose billions on its pulpwood timber reserves and its control of the paper market with woodpulp-sulfide paper. DuPont stood to lose billions on their acid-rain-producing, forest-stripping, woodpulp-sulfide patents. The third party in position to gain or lose was their banker, Andrew Mellon, Secretary of the Treasury. Whether by conspiracy or coincidence, these three united to become the major force to get marijuana prohibited by the government. In 1931, Mellon appointed his nephew Harry Anslinger Director of the new Federal Bureau of Narcotics (formerly his beer-busting G-Men) to crusade against "the demon weed." Before Congress, Anslinger's testimony was almost entirely Hearst newspaper releases read aloud in the emotionally-charged style of the exaggerated or contrived news called "yellow journalism." He declared marijuana the worst violence-inducing substance known, and implied its use (and not social injustice) was responsible for the well-known violent tendencies of the Negro and Latin. The culmination of the attack was the film "Reefer Madness," which time has revealed to be ludicrous. On the basis of that mentality, however, marijuana was outlawed. DuPont and Hearst in a single move wiped out their major competitor in paper, textiles, and paint. Treasury Secretary Andrew Mellon was no doubt pleased to deposit the fruits of their good fortune into their accounts at the Mellon Bank of Pittsburgh, which he happened to own.

Curiously, not only petroleum products increased in value by outlawing hemp. In Kentucky the useful crop was replaced by tobacco, which has no use except as a drug, no medicinal use, and has been admitted by the government to be a leading cause of death in America. For millennia, marijuana has been one of the most used herbs in traditional medicine, and from 1850 to 1937 it appeared in American pharmacopeia recommended for dozens of maladies. Testifying against the 1937 Marijuana Tax Act, representatives of the American Medical Association (AMA) declared, "…it is all a Hearst media scare intended to control Mexicans and Negroes, and once the active ingredients are isolated, it will likely be the miracle drug of the age." However, medical research on the possible benefits of marijuana were forbidden by the US Government until 1961, when Anslinger retired as Director of the Bureau of Narcotics.

In 1976, Eli Lilly and other drug manufacturers lobbied to outlaw all independent research into the medical potential of marijuana. In return, they promised to undertake development of synthetic THC they could patent, expecting the same benefits without the "abusable" high of the real thing. Lilly came out with Nabulone, a synthetic which did not produce the high, or any of the other effects of the natural product. It was never marketed, and after twenty-five years of research, drugmakers have not succeeded in creating a synthetic which works as well as the free-growing weed. Having the only research franchise the government is going to issue, they likely never will, no matter how long they keep trying. Until forced to admit they have exhausted every possibility, they need not resort to considering the merits of the natural substance, and they do not have to face loss of their "windfall" monopoly. Marijuana is an excellent mild analgesic, relaxant, and tranquilizer. It is the best for relief of intra-ocular eye pressure due to glaucoma. It is an excellent bronchial dilator. Unlike Valium, Librium, Thorazine, Prozac, and other such synthetic drugs, it has no toxic side effects, and it creates no physiological dependence. Unlike each of those manufactured attempts to create a safe mood lifter, its prolonged use produces no harmful withdrawal symptoms, other than irritability and loss of appetite for up to a week. Unlike each of those unnatural molecules, the purest THC can be grown free everywhere in America, and consumed raw in salads, smoked, or extracted as a drinkable tincture in any kitchen. If legal, it would replace a large part of the market for those profitable other substances, a market in the billions of dollars. Such were the findings of the US Costa Rican Studies, 1982, according to a copy of the original report sent to offices of NORML in 1983. The final report on the studies, the version accepted by NIH and the Reagan administration after rewriting it themselves, was a vague document offering only generalities and inconclusive summaries.

Hemp is not only valuable as medicine, and a fiber and oil source, but also is an excellent source of food. Hemp seed is second only to soybeans as a complete vegetable protein source. It is highest in certain enzymes and amino acids of any grain, and is less expensive to produce than soybeans. Using hemp seed as a byproduct of hemp fiber production, domestic animals and livestock could be fed for less than feeds now in common use. According to USDA, hemp is one of the best re-nitrogenizing rotation crops, and will grow in many regions where no other crop can profitably survive. Many Third World countries today could solve both their food problem and dependence on petroleum-based products by growing hemp. How does the US Government react to that news? By a systematic program of misinformation, suppression of positive evidence, and deliberate omission of the truth in presenting the subject to the American people, students, legislators, and the world. In the Third World, US foreign aid, loans, and military aid are directly tied to the willingness of leaders to impose restrictive drug control over their people. When American-imposed raids on their private lives cause those people to voice their objections, CIA and DEA are sent in to identify rebellious anti-government drug traffickers. The first time a dissenter points out that the ones who profit by the action are the American capitalists, he is declared a leftist, and the military advisors are called in. When somebody voices his objection loudly enough, he is called a terrorist, and America sends in the Security Fleet. Nations which submit themselves and their people to the anti-drug activity find their fields sprayed with paraquat, which the American government knows is poisonous, and their citizens rounded up and searched by armed troops.

The heirs of the Mellon, Hearst, and DuPont conspiracy don't want people to know about the beneficial aspects of marijuana, but they do want people to know about the law-enforcement problem, and its effect on the morality of their children. When powerful people in position to profit persuade legislators to make marijuana a felony, they may then assert that marijuana is making felons of our children, and nothing must be spared to protect them from that. Regardless what may be said about the desirability of marijuana as a recreational drug, it is clear that the benefits of the many products of hemp far outweigh whatever harmful effects have been documented in the many decades of study of this plant. Unfortunately, it is precisely because of the ability of hemp products to perform successfully against several powerful competing industries that it is kept illegal, and likely will be for the proximate future. Like cartoonist Al Capp's altruistic Schmoos, Cannabis provides too freely what others would prefer exclusive right to sell.

A Drug-War
Questionnaire #1

Consider these options, which face young adults in our town today. Let's say they saved allowances and birthday presents, and now have a High School diploma and $1000. A: They can put the money into savings, and after one year, will have made about $50. B: They can put $800 into a used car, spend $200 on wardrobe, and get a minimum-wage job. After deductions and costs, they can take home about $100 a week. C: They can buy a pound of marijuana, sell ounces at $100 hanging out with friends, and double the money in a couple of months. (All they have to do is conceal their lives from parents, educators, pastors, and any officer of any agency of the government of The United States of America.) QUESTION: If we are trying to create a drug-free family-oriented patriotic community, what could be stupider than making drug-dealing the easiest way for young people to get money, while thereby turning them into criminals who distrust anyone in public office? // Our government made marijuana illegal declaring it too dangerous to let the citizen make up his own mind. Tobacco, cause of heart and lung disease, is the leading cause of death, killing more people than all other drugs, war and murder thrown in too. If we outlawed cigarettes today, would the result be fewer smokers, or more criminals? Would it prevent folks from growing it—or would good citizens in North Carolina protect their families' secrets…for a piece of the action. If a pack of cigarettes cost fifty bucks—about what the same amount of marijuana costs today—a suitcase full would be worth about twenty-five grand. People become black-marketers, robbers, even murderers for that much loot. QUESTION: Would it be fair to say tobacco caused those crimes? Are the tragedies, the crimes, and the punishments of the dope business the result of the smoke…or the heat? // The decisions are made by our most senior policy makers—from the President down. However, if a candidate for President, Congress, the Supreme Court, or DEA stands up and says, "I tried marijuana myself," that candidate is declared morally unfit for office. If a candidate for the Farm Bureau revealed he had never been a farmer; if a candidate for Secretary of Defense had never been a soldier or seen war; if a candidate for Trade Commissioner had never held a job, wouldn't we say they were incompetent? Yet when it comes to drugs, a primary requirement for making the decisions which affect the lives of not just drug users, but all of us, is a confession of total lack of first-hand knowledge. Our zero-tolerance policy has placed us all in the hands of the deliberately uninformed. What is worse, they consider themselves therefore morally superior. QUESTION: If trust in authority, and personal ignorance of the subject are requisite for getting the drug-regulation jobs, how can we expect results other than dictatorial policy based on incompetent opinion? // An ounce of marijuana at $100 is about the standard size purchase. It will make about fifty joints, and last from two weeks to a month. If you smoked it all at once, you would probably wake up with your mouth tasting like hippies camped there all night. A standard prescription purchase of Seconal, Qualuud, Placidyl, Nembutal, or Tuinal may run the same general price, intended to last about the same time. These drugs cure no illness, and are intended to provide the same thing the pothead seeks—mood control, relaxation, freedom from anxiety, and sleep. But if you take all of a single purchase at once, any of those listed could kill you. The pot-peddler is locked up, stripped of liberty, voting franchise, security clearance, bondability, insurability, pilot's license, firearm ownership, and whatever property or vehicles he may own. The pill-pusher is a respected citizen with a secure income. QUESTION: Why are the illegal drugs only those which can be grown and used without a manufacturer, inspector, packager, wholesaler, physician, pharmacist, and tax collector? Are marijuana, opium, and the like banned because they grow free—and none of those guys get their protected piece of the action? // America imprisons the highest percentage of its population. Dockets are backed up months, prisons jammed, and costs of more prisons go up and up. For disobedience to laws against self-abuse, relatively innocent lambs are forced to lie down with lions—literally, sometimes. The naive young adult who goes into prison for selling dope to his friend is likely to come out a bitter sophisticated criminal. The cost to the taxpayer of that destructive incarceration is higher than the average national wage. QUESTION: To relieve our courts and jails of a huge burden, and to stop turning small-time "self-abusers" into seasoned ex-cons, how about asking for a blanket Presidential pardon for all offenders now in jail for possession, distribution, and use of drugs? We could rent the vacated prison space to our friends in Singapore, whose zero-tolerance policies have recently included chewing gum.

A Drug-War
Questionnaire #2

Same song, second verse; could get better, but more likely worse. Is the medicine worse than the disease? Prosecuting users has not stopped drug use, but instead has created a global criminal industry. Using drugs will not of itself make a person dangerous to society. Suffering years in prison for so-called self-abuse can make an angry, anti-social person of almost anyone. Prisons are universities for crime, and many who go in as petty drug offenders come out bitter sophisticated criminals. Because drug users are defined as criminals, millions of Americans see themselves as outside the law, and they view the US Government as an irrational and oppressive force to be feared and hated. What could drugs themselves possibly do to be worse for a nation than that? QUESTION: Isn't using enforced prohibition to treat drug abuse like using a power sander to treat acne? It gets rid of the zits, all right, but... // Prohibition drives prices up, making drugs the most valuable crop in countries where they grow, and the peasants' only chance at rising above poverty, thereby disrupting their economies. It virtually guarantees that everyone who can grow it will do so. Having lured them into the drug market with our consumers' money, America then uses taxpayers' money to force them out of it by paying the local General to send troops to control them by force. The opportunity for the General to take over the drug market, and thus control the country, is obvious. If our foreign policy is supposed to be based on promoting democracy and free enterprise, how could we do worse than take actions which encourage corrupt military police regimes in the Third World? QUESTION: Is America morally justified in arming foreign governments against their own people to prevent Americans from "self-abuse"? // Would the death sentence for drug dealing stop the traffic? Put fifty thousand dollars and a briefcase of cocaine into the same secret room, and it draws predators like flies. Lots of folks will kill for that much loot, and for a major dealer to know the US government is officially adding itself to the list is merely an ironic footnote to the accepted risks of business. One certain result would be increased violence. Most dealers are not killer psychos, but ordinary folks, and if they get busted, they take their lumps and do their time. But if a bust meant a death sentence, they would have nothing to lose by trying to kill the arresting officer. QUESTION: Would making drug-dealing a capital crime be an effective deterrent, or just a death sentence for the working cop? // One killer put six bullets into a person for a forbidden sexual relation. A second killer put six bullets into a person for burning The Flag. Another killer put six bullets into a person over a drug deal. Was the first killer justified, because of morality—or was it lustful jealousy which led him to declare murder a fair wage for infidelity? Was the second killer justified, because of patriotism—or was it bigoted pride that led him to judge, sentence, and execute? As for the third killer, the motives most likely are simple greed, or payback for betrayal. Those motives are not caused by drugs. They are unavoidable elements of doing business in any highly-desired commodity forbidden by law. Making drugs legal will not stop people from killing for greed, nor for lust, pride, nor recreation. But it would stop people from killing each other for drugs. QUESTION: Is there something special about drugs that makes it worse to commit a crime because of them, than to commit the same crime for some other reason? // The natural drugs, opium, cocaine, and marijuana are not the only ones which can be abused. The most dangerous are manufactured as medicine. Though controlled by prescription, they are made in quantities far exceeding our prescription need. The extras are sold to other countries, then brought back into the US as black-market street drugs—Seconal, Tuinal, Qaaluud, Placidyl, and Amytal, to name a few which are lethal if overdosed. QUESTION: To stop the deadly flow of black-market pharmaceuticals on the streets, why not attack them at the source by making it a crime for the "licensed kingpins" to make more than our prescription need calls for? // The drug problem must be solved, but violent enforcement of prohibition has not and cannot solve the problem—it is in itself another problem, much more destructive than the drugs themselves. When a government institutes totalitarian measures, it becomes a tyranny, no matter how sincerely it was brought to that state. When permitted to bloom, tyranny can be brought down only by the horror and tragedy of internal violence. If we would halt the destruction of American civil freedom, and the plunge toward the tyranny of police-state bureaucracy, we must stop the War on Drugs now. "There was an old woman who swallowed a fly…." You remember what happened to her.

FAA: Just
Another DEA Tool

Cannot someone establish a Maximum Authorized Altitude on the height of bureaucratic folly? Aircraft Owners and Pilots Association (AOPA), the largest general aviation organization, recently published figures provided by the Federal Aviation Administration (FAA) and the National Transportation Safety Board (NTSB) listing the major causes of aircraft accidents: poor pilot judgement, weather, structural or system failure, and so forth. Where are the figures which reveal the most critical cause of aircraft accidents is really drugs? Where are any data which conclusively show drugs to be a significant causal factor in any aircraft accident? If there are no such figures, then why was FAA pressured to be first in line with a Federal Aviation Regulation (FAR) calling for mandatory testing of pilots and other aviation professionals for illegal drugs in the name of increasing the safety of flying? Please spare me such leaps of reason as, "Cocaine was found in the pilot's corpse; the drug is illegal because it is dangerous; therefore drugs caused the accident." Please also spare me the conclusion, "An illegal drug caused the accident; the pilot was thus criminally negligent; therefore, the pilot's employer has to pay all the damages." Having taken those huge leaps, it becomes all too easy for employers to rationalize their all-too-reasonable fear of liability suit by further concluding,

"Aviation safety is therefore best promoted by mandatory drug testing of everyone who flies for a living." Since employers would rather not take the blame for demanding the tests, and one can only blame so much on the insurance companies, they would certainly prefer the order to come from some other desk. FAA was the expedient tool.

Pilots, however, are one of the worker groups least likely to be using the drugs which are the declared objects of the testing program. They are likely to be more safety-conscious, health-conscious, and self-disciplined than most others. Yet pilots (and their Air Traffic Controller counterparts) were the first group of workers singled out as without question having the job most severely mandating drug tests. If the generals of the "drug war" were looking for a group with a high likelihood of drug use while controlling public transportation vehicles which have an extremely high accident rate, the obvious top offender is automobiles—so why was there no clamor to make drug testing mandatory for cab drivers? Aviation's safety record is excellent, by any standard which could be applied to American industry across the board—and pilots operate in one of the more dangerous environments. Their professional standards are very high, despite all the media fear-mongering about incompetent pilots. The skeptical non-flier is invited to try putting the next couple of years into earning the Commercial-Instrument Pilot rating needed just to submit an application for airline training. To select pilots as the group most needing drug policing to ensure safety on the job is an insult to one of America's finest professional corps.

Then why was it done? If safety were truly the goal, the concern might more sensibly be with those drugs more likely to be used by pilots and more likely to cause interference with their ability. Those are their prescription sleeping aids, pain killers, and tranquilizers. However, those are not the subject of the tests. The tests are looking for marijuana, opiates, amphetamines, and cocaine, the big-bucks black market stuff. It is all too easy to infer this was never really an aviation safety matter, but a Drug Enforcement Agency program pursued for the sake of establishing an enforcement precedent. But why pilots? Because they are a group whose low level of use would probably produce a low level of protest, a group already accustomed to high levels of professional regulation. They are also a group associated with a high level of social paranoia. In spite of favorable statistics, lots of people still fear flying, and would vote to have pilots lobotomized and implanted with Mode-C Attitude Adjustors if they thought it would ease their discomfort at seeing another airplaneful of people spread across forty acres of newspaper headline.

If those who seek to increase government surveillance and control over Americans in the name of the Drug War had to take mandatory drug testing of anyone to the Supreme Court, the proposal would likely fail. By slipping it in as a Federal Aviation Regulation, which is not a law, they bypass all the legislative bodies. Making drug testing an FAR requirement was successful use of the FAA as the tool of another agency for a purpose of questionable legality. If anybody in a position of critical responsibility "needs" drug testing on the job, then let us begin with the Congress. They could be expected to claim immunity, proclaiming the Constitution of this free country protects them from such egregious invasion of their personal lives with a tool intended only to protect the citizen from degenerate criminals on drugs.

Who Wants Cancer Cured?

What if researchers discovered the cure for cancer is marijuana? Would the American Medical Association rejoice that lives could be spared and expensive procedures unnecessary if tobacco smokers all switched to hemp? Would the pharmaceutical industry rejoice to know the drugs they make to "treat" dying cancer patients at any cost might be replaced by a common herb grown free as cabbage anywhere in America? Would the Surgeon General proclaim the discovery and call for the right of Americans to grow and use the herb to protect their health? Would the Attorney General demand Congress stop the insanity of prosecuting the cure of a disease caused by the tobacco they cynically subsidize and greedily tax? Would Congress rise up cheering to give back to the people the Constitutional rights they have "needed" to take away so law enforcement might more efficiently bag marijuana users? Would the President stand up (as Libertarian candidate Harry Browne promised to do) and issue a blanket pardon for everyone now in prison on marijuana "self-abuse" charges? Might he even restore the voting rights of the millions disenfranchised as marijuana felons since Nixon invented the term "War On Drugs" trying to cop spin off Johnson's War On Poverty? Would the agents, administrators, and sub-contractors of the DEA, FBI, ATF, CIA, INS, and ETC of the FED, the Marshals, Sheriffs, Police, and schoolyard "safety" officers —not to mention the legions of prosecutors and dopewar defense lawyers—rejoice that they were no longer required to bear the burden of imposing marijuana prohibition by force on otherwise peaceful and productive citizens in America and all the other nations in which the "soldiers" of our War On Drugs are doing what soldiers do? Would they rejoice that large parts of their budgets, activities, and staff might not be necessary at all? Would they appreciate that their jobs might be harder without the otherwise-unconstitutional powers given to them in the name of protecting Americans from evil and destructive marijuana? Would stockholders and employees of the increasingly-privatized rapid-growth penal industry be pleased to see the cell blocks of their huge new state "correction and rehabilitation" facilities standing empty, and contracts for bigger ones canceled? Would the Marijuana Growers Association rejoice to see the price of their product fall from $100 for half an ounce to the same price as half an ounce of tobacco—that is, one pack of cigarettes? The market for recreational and medicinal marijuana and hemp products would thrive as competitive agriculture, but wouldn't the professional outlaw drop the product like PeeWee Herman, since there's not enough markup in legitimate trade, and farming is such damn hard work?

Or might all those folks find it reasonable and expedient to encourage the President to suppress the report of the discovery, to place all research on marijuana into the hands of the drug companies, and to vigorously prosecute the War on Drugs? Come on, this is cancer we're talking about, number one killer of Americans. Surely no sane and responsible person could do such a thing, much less our trusted Presidents. Would you believe this has already happened? And not just once?

Raymond Cushing <http://www.alternet.org/story.html?StoryID=9257> reports researchers in Madrid have successfully destroyed brain cancer in rats with THC, the active ingredient in marijuana. They also tested to see if THC caused behavior problems, or any damage. They found no damage except to the cancer. No major US newspaper covered the story, which appeared once on the AP news wire, Feb. 29th. It is not the first time this has been discovered. In 1974, researchers at The Medical College of Virginia, funded by NIH to find evidence marijuana damages the immune system, found instead that THC slowed the growth of lung cancer and breast cancer. DEA shut down the Virginia study and in 1976, President Ford outlawed public marijuana research and granted exclusive research rights to certain pharmaceutical companies. Rather than confirm the herb's value, they set out to develop a synthetic (that is, patentable) THC to deliver the medical benefits without the "immoral" high which justifies keeping the free natural plant illegal. They are still asking for more time. In 1983, Reagan tried to force the universities to destroy all 1966-76 marijuana research data, including compendiums in libraries. Clinton fired his Surgeon General for suggesting renewed discussion of marijuana. Bush II supports a "meth-lab" bill to make it illegal to even link your computer to a website on which information about illegal drugs is published. It might be a crime to have read this. Legalize marijuana? Cure cancer? How could we even consider it—too many people have too much to lose.

"Annie, (we're here to) Get Your Gun!"

"You can take my gun when you pry my dead finger off the trigger. (PS: I won't save the last bullet for myself. I'll shoot one more fascist and die a free man.") These sentiments feel really great, especially for the veteran or immigrant who has seen the elephant up close. The same also feel genuine horror watching Americans disarmed physically and mentally by such anti-gun activism as the elimination of rifle training from High School ROTC, and the marketing of gun fear by media and political exploiters.

No government which feels it must arm itself against its citizens may rightly call itself a democracy, no matter what charades are played out on C-SPAN in the name of free elections. No zealous authoritarian bureaucracy in history has proved immune to the tragedy of statist power turned inward against its own people. In countries that have been our enemies, our allies, and our families' homelands, millions have been disarmed, rounded up, and exterminated as political, racial, religious, or behavioral undesirables. When our Founding Fathers wrote the Second Amendment, they did so openly declaring it was to protect the citizens' ability to defend themselves from tyrannous use of the power of government by those in office. Though it is horrifying to even consider having to take up arms against a US-Fed-Gone-Wrong, they believed from personal experience the best way to prevent that was to guarantee the right of every citizen to possess the means to do so. The Constitution uses the word "arms." Though there may be other types of guns, knives, and explosives, that word means specifically those things intended for lethal combat with other human beings. One does not "bear arms" against ducks and deer, even if hunting them with an assault rifle. The argument that registered sporting rifles fulfill our Constitutional right to possess armament is mental sleight-of-hand to divert attention from the Second Amendment's purpose.

Nonetheless, the issue of keeping arms for defense against the Fed is moot. The position is not defensible. To know a felony is in progress and not report it is a crime called misprision. Those who know their neighbors possess felonious weapons are obligated by law to report them. Using Zero Tolerance policies like the War On Drugs, any such report may be used to authorize no-knock invasion of any home by "peace officers" armed and mentally prepared to defend themselves from the weapon they have come to get. Likewise, any registered gun belongs to the State. The right authorities sign the right paper of permission, and an agent with a badge comes to take it. Refuse loudly, and you are called potential terrorist, and surrounded. Refuse strongly, and they send in the Waco vets and the B-52's—and that don't mean Fred Schneider's band. Therein lies the fallacy of the anti-tyranny argument for keeping personal military arms. Even if kept by patriotic local militia, rifles, even tanks could only be used in a futile gesture of self-sacrifice. That produces only increased Federal paranoia, and thus increased justification for oppressive measures used against the common citizen.

More important today is the right of the citizen to arm himself against aggression by other citizens. Unfortunately, that right is all too often abused by some Americans, and all too often needed by others. Attempts by the fearful bourgeois to make the abuse impossible through prohibition of personal self-defense only make the lawful citizen more vulnerable to predation, and more subject to authoritarian security measures. When personal defense weapons are banned, and the good sheep obey, then outlaws and police both become more heavily armed and confrontational. The lawful citizen has neither peace nor security, but armed antagonists on both sides, one imprisoning him to protect him from the other.

All rhetoric aside, the most pragmatic point of view seems clear. If the sane and free man knows he must go where his life is at risk, and he believes a pistol concealed in his jock will defend his life, it likely does not matter to him what opinion about his right to arm himself is held by the Sheriff, the Congress, Bill Clinton, Rosie O'Donnell, or the Pope. If he faces a gang of street predators, then anyone who tries by law to take away his pistol is simply another obstacle to his survival. To accede to the authority of their opinions, or submit to their threats of prosecution, and therefore give up the weapon could be seen as psychotic denial of the real threat he knows he faces, and therefore an irrational suicidal act. He might more sanely justify the juridical risks of carrying the forbidden weapon by saying, "I would rather be tried by twelve than carried by six."

A Government Bird-Safety Program

"Who governs least governs best." Certainly there is or ought to be some part of our lives in which government governs not at all. Off hand, I cannot think of one area of human experience about which the official position of the United States Federal, State, and Local Government is, "That is none of our business." To protect us from cheating each other, the government has outlawed free trade between citizens, making every transaction the subject of regulation and tax. To protect us from sinful self-abuse, the government has presumed mandatory stewardship over our bodies, regulating which drugs are forbidden, and which may not be refused, and enforcing their prescription with surveillance at the molecular level, and control at the lethal level. To protect us from robbing and killing each other, the government is taking away our right to defend ourselves from each other, and turning the peace officer corps into a military occupation force. There is little point in wailing about the fact that all of what were once called our Constitutional rights and freedoms are in practice long gone. All of our rights have been taken from us in the name of government responsibility to keep us protected from ourselves.

It is not possible to teach a bird to fly with safety guaranteed. If it were intended to be so, then God would have given birds parachutes. I wrote that like a joke, but I have some trepidation about it. I fear some cow-eyed bird-loving compulsive do-goodie will be moved to petition his senator to do something about the plight of our nation's eaglets, and she will decide the answer is a new branch of the Interior, responsible for retrofitting every eaglet with a parachute before it attempts the potentially-fatal act of flying. When it makes the TV news and starts selling tabloid woodpulp-and-ink and some airtime, the Senate starts the money flowing, the spin-doctors twirl their press agents, and the Federengi in the coke-filled back rooms play their master game of contacts, contracts, and gold-pressed latinum. Operation Safe Eagle is passed and funded to rousing cheers in the halls of Congress. The do-goodie gets to sleep in the Lincoln Bedroom. Everybody is happy.

There is only one problem. It will take several fiscal years to award the contracts, do the research, develop programs, and to invent, test, approve, manufacture, and implement the fail-safe Federal feather-chutes. Meanwhile, the eaglets are risking their lives, and as the government has accepted responsibility for the safety of the birds, it feels obligated to take authoritative action to eliminate the risk. Someone quickly points out that the technology to protect the fledglings is already available. We have only to send out Federal Officers—such as the Forest Rangers—to put safety cages around all the nests to keep the birds from jumping out until their feather-chutes arrive. Think that's a joke too? There was a time when School Safety Programs were conducted by the School Nurse. Today that term describes the activities of armed law-enforcement officers employing both high-tech and hands-on investigative and control measures, and reporting to a staff of "disciplinary care-providers" in the Dean's office. They may do something to help safety, but they are enforcing obedience to a laundry-list of behavioral regulations, from totalitarian submission to drug policing to dress and language codes. Using procedures borrowed from the DA's office, they make top grades in categorizing each student's violations of other students' safety, filling out the forms, and administering the appropriate punishment, confident in the prime axiom of the bureaucracy, "If the paperwork is right, the act is right." The result is safety-cage schools, which for all the justifying rhetoric about the necessity, are nonetheless in practice run like penal institutions.

The function of government should most correctly be to establish and protect the rights and freedoms of each individual. Given such freedom, each individual should most correctly devote himself to the common good. Isn't that what we are taught America is about, the voluntary cooperation of free people? But people are only as free as their neighbors agree to respect their rights. If you cannot leave home without being mugged or burglarized, it does not matter what the laws say. If people do not respect each others rights, it does not matter if government grants them. If neighbors steal each others property, soon none of them have any. If they will not even respect each others lives, then even the best (or worst) police cannot save them by building protective birdcages around their lives.

It is not possible to teach a bird to fly in a cage. Those who will not be broken will destroy the cage if they must to get out, or they will destroy themselves against its bars, or against each other. Those who survive at best can only walk, and must be fed by agents of other government programs.

Educating Jailbirds

In the history of America, nothing has been more destructive to the nation than our own War On Drugs, which has caused more damage to citizens, to our legal rights, our business practices, our communities, our foreign policy, and to the trust between citizens and the state, many times more damage than all the drugs this persecution is intended to prohibit. Even so, perhaps the most destructive effects are yet to be seen, the results of anti-drug measures in the public school. Many government agencies have been made tools of DEA, since regulation and policy may be written at will, and need not fulfill the requirements of becoming duly-passed laws—yet may be fully enforced. These agencies include the INS, IRS, FAA, FDA, ATF, FCC, CIA, DOL, DOT, ETC… all given roles and powers which exist only to enable greater surveillance and control of us all for drug interdiction, whatever the agency's nominal field of authority. Nothing more quickly arouses the willingness of the fearful sheep to surrender their power and rights to the sheepdogs than the cry to "protect the innocent children." Their media-stimulated fear of the dangers of the world (and their ecclesiastogenic revulsion for the "immoral") has enabled the drug fascists to impose practices in the schools which would be considered Stalinesque if declared as political policy, but which are accepted as anti-drug security measures. Our public schools are operated in the manner of penal institutions. School safety program designers are trained in police science. High school students are locked in, subject to restrictions enforced by uniformed armed guards. Though use of "obscene language" to an officer is a statutory crime, campus police exercise force to impose obedience. To ensure each suspicious student is free of drugs and weapons, they may sieze, arrest, and intimately search any dirty-mouth perp who speaks ill to authority. Though parent conference is mandatory, the system of campus discipline is not negotiable, but is a summary prosecution, to which the parent has only the principal to appeal. Administration finds it expedient for order's sake to look the other way, or to participate enthusiastically in running a clean, safe, moral, and well-disciplined school.

Whether this policy is "right" or not, there are inescapable consequences of raising our children in a prison-like environment. If they are treated like prisoners—even for their own good—they will learn to think like prisoners, and to see themselves as prisoners. Since many are more sophisticated in real life than the schools' behavioral policies let them acknowledge on campus, they recognize the state is imposing restrictive illusions upon them. They might conclude the freedom of reality lies in escaping state oppression, and opposing those who support it. Raising kids in jail produces three kinds of adults: guards, inmates, and outlaws. Then we wonder why the ones that blow up the place are the smart ones from good homes... Public school is a mandatory term of incarceration in a state institution, under armed guard and physical duress. While being presented technical information and historical indoctrination, students are subject to behavioral regimentation to enforce the primary datum of the syllabus: belief in the rightness of and obedience to the authority of the state. Those who do not easily submit may be placed on mood-altering medication, and to refuse that is a crime. When practiced by other governments, placing the youth in mandatory behavior conditioning camps and using force, drugs, and propaganda to get them to obey The Leader is commonly called brainwashing.

Can the school system be fixed? No. Its problems are fundamental. The drugwar use of penal security in schools is only one of its fatal flaws. Another is federal requirements based on demographic academic statistics. Funding statistics have become the primary concern of administrators, which has led to breakdown of standards of academic excellence. Affirmative-action labor policies have further made the academic part of the education experience meaningless to the working-class student. Where authoritarian moralists predominate, schools obligate students to posture in obedience to puritanical dress, language, and behavior codes far different from their real lives, further alienating them. Is the system therefore going to collapse? Not soon. If someday we just dispense with The Constitution altogether, and elevate some four-star Drug Czar to the White House with the authority to get the job done, the system evolving in public education today might be the salvation of those young enough to still have innocence to protect. And for those malcontents who just couldn't take the yoke? Well, school is after all an introduction to the penal system. "We've got just the place you're trained to be, Boy. Wh'say we start you off with three to five for that bag of dope?"

Student Chores:
Child Abuse?

According to recent outcry in the news, the condition of school buildings in some areas of our country is so bad that it is deemed impossible for any student to be expected to learn anything at all therein. To solve such an inexcusable and opprobrious offense against our most valuable national resource of raw material, our children, the conventional wisdom must surely be to form a civic activist group to lobby the legislators to propose a study to float a bond to fund the school districts to employ a contractor to administer a program to hire an institutional sanitation engineering and physical plant maintenance specialist to write a multi-lingual manual of protocol and instruction to be used as a syllabus in a study group program to upgrade the skills of the administrators of the supervisors of the janitor whose job is to clean the place up. Such a program should surely be augmented by a new division of the State Zero-Tolerance Policy Administration (the most brilliant and indispensable addition to national education since Gutenberg's press) to assure that no student be permitted to commit such anti-education acts as dropping fast-food containers left from their healthful and delicious Nutrition-Department-approved cafeteria meals, without appropriate action taken by the Dean's Office to ensure that the prerequisite paperwork be impeccably completed to assign such appropriate punishment as suspension from classes, and that the responsible parent or guardian be mandatorily invited to meet with that Disciplinary Care Provider to lead his or her child in the correct rituals of obeisance before such duly-constituted authority.

In my albeit long-past training as a Marine and as an Army officer, I learned that the first step toward self-discipline is keeping oneself and one's surroundings clean. It seems to me that people can be distinguished as part of the problem or part of the solution by observing their behavior: some leave every situation they enter a little worse than they found it, something consumed, and something messy left behind, while others leave every room they enter a little cleaner than they found it, with something added, or something a little less disordered. In school our student are taught that the government's system is expected to provide everything ready for them to consume, and then to clean it all up while they are home watching meaningful Federally-regulated programs on TV. Worse, in our numerous public programs of social welfare and concern for the well-being of the disadvantaged, the prevailing opinion is that if persons belong to the correct demographic categories, they have a "right" to complain if it isn't done well enough to satisfy them, or to take what they deserve from anyone who appears to have it, or to express their understandable angst in righteous acts of civil violence. How could such attitudes instill in our children the desire to be among the cleaners and providers, instead of feeling most at home among the thoughtless consumers and the recreational vandals?

It seems to me there is one obvious solution to both the immediate problem of school building condition, and the long-range problem of instilling in our youth a sense of personal responsibility for the cleanliness of their surroundings. Dare I suggest that custodial skills and building maintenance be made a mandatory course of instruction in our schools, and each student obligated to a daily period of housekeeping duties? What if elementary students at recess were graded for bringing from the playground the odd bits of paper, bottle caps, cigarette butts, condom wrappers, and the like which comprise the common windblown detritus of the campuses of our cities? How soon in a child's development might it be possible to instruct him or her in the proper use of a push-broom, without abusing that child's rights, or violating the child-labor laws? Whether or not the school teaches its boys construction skills, or its girls household skills, at what point in a citizen's education might it be possible to safely teach the procedure to any boy or girl for replacing a fluorescent light-bulb, a blown electrical fuse, or a broken windowpane? Does one need a vocational-school curriculum to learn the complicated technique of operating a floor-buffer? Might a student who has demonstrated his expertise in the use of a spray-paint can to artistically tag a wall not be shown how to use the same street-wise talent to upgrade the condition of a scratched metal desk? Do we need to fund and build such magnet-school masterpieces as the Academy of Custodial Service Arts and International Neatness, or could just any good old country school actually be provided with the proper Federal and State wisdom and leadership to impart such skill and depth of character to our otherwise clueless progeny? And furthermore (not to frighten anyone with radical revolutionary concepts), what if (gasp!) the teachers even assigned homework?

They Can't Fix The Schools

Can the public school system be "fixed"? No. It's problems are fundamental, and more of the same will only make it worse. More money will only make it fail faster. Giving moralist authoritarian administrators more power will only make it more destructive to the children, and ultimately, to the nation. Gerrymandering curriculum and academic standards to produce politically-correct statistics for funding and propaganda lead to lower levels of student performance. Public school is a government-run industry to turn raw material—children—into input products needed by other industry: uniformly propagandized, unthinkingly obedient worker/consumers. Struggling to contain a sophisticated and aware generation, schools have become prep-schools for prison, statist propaganda mills masquerading as academic institutions by forcing students to maintain the illusion of pre-adolescent Sunday-school day camps.

The biggest offenders? Self-appointed moral police, drug warriors protecting the children from self-abuse, self-righteous zealots protecting them from knowledge of and opportunity to sin, and from the heresy of empiricism. Wet-eyed Pollyannas who believe enforcing ignorance in the name of defending innocence is better for youth than helping them gain access to all of the truth, and the wisdom to use their right to make their own decisions about it. Parents and other citizens willing to demand schools not only educate their children, but toilet train, and teach them basic social skills they do not or can not give them at home. To raise the children for them.

The unfortunate result of the government's willingness to do so is that the parent who objects to the system's judgements and procedures quickly finds he has no authority to place his own chosen teachings and values before those of the school in the upbringing of his child. The result of government presuming the responsibility and power of raising all the children denies the right of all parents to pass on their own ways, from the most deeply committed Pentecostal to the most libertine Libertarian. All of US.

The first fundamental change which would be necessary to "fix" the school system: public school must not be mandatory, but a voluntary opportunity. The parent or young person who prefers to choose some other path to destiny should be absolutely free to do so. The notion that the child must be industrially skilled and drilled in the history and doctrine of the state, even if by criminalizing the parent, is not a policy befitting any nation associating itself with the word *freedom*, but is cruel tyranny over the minds of its citizens, at the time when we are most trusting and vulnerable. Adding insult to cruelty is that as the student being indoctrinated in the proclaimed ideology of the state, The Constitution, grows in awareness, he sees (but is forced to behave as though he did not) that the practices of the government are anything but Constitutional. This awareness does not lead the believer in those principles to become loyal to the government. It follows then, that those most likely to be loyal to the system are either still living within the illusion they were taught, or they believe the Constitutional principles inferior to more authoritarian social structures such as the welfare police state. If the attendance in government-regulated school is mandatory upon punishment by incarceration, and imposing that "government benefit" enforced by the techniques of high security and correctionalism, then by any name, the school is a prison.

The next most important change is to eliminate the concept of age-determined or time-determined progress. The public education system should be open from its most elementary classes to anyone of any age or background for whom the level of the subject matter is relevant. An illiterate adult of thirty, or an immigrant seeking citizenship, should be able to take second-grade reading if that is his level of need; a twelve-year-old able to meaningfully address hieroglyphic should be admitted to any class of her intellectual peers. The key to progress must be mastery of the subject, at any level. That means not only do we dispense with forced age-grouping, we make progression totally dependent on ability to demonstrate 100% fluency with 100% of the syllabus. No sliding by with your age group with C's indicating you learned half of the subject. When you have all the answers, you pass, whether it takes you six weeks or six years. Nobody says you have to pass to get another birthday or a job, but until you get it all, you can't take the next course in the program. Though classes might have members of many ages and social backgrounds, they would have in common that they were all at the same level with respect to the subject. Some Americans would graduate at 16, and some at 61, but they would be the best.

NOT For The Children

Letting the public school system "fix" itself will not work, no matter how much money is poured into it, nor how much power over students and parents school administrators are given by politicians, moralist authoritarian board members, and sectarian activists. We need a supersonic multi-directional omni-targetable fleet, so letting them retool their battleship won't solve the fundamental problems. No solution can be made until we become honest about the purpose of public education. When attendance behind locked doors is mandatory to the minute, dress and behavior codes rigidly enforced to impose a uniform puritanical image, and safety concerns motivate penal-science methods of security and discipline, it becomes difficult to continue to accept the rhetoric that public education is a program operated at taxpayers expense for the benefit of the children and society. What is school really for? Every teacher, administrator, and security officer on every campus in the country will quickly affirm (with hand on heart and eyes glazed over) that the formal education, intellectual development, and personal growth of each individual student is the sole purpose of the entire system. Unfortunately, in spite of their desire or belief, it is simply not true. Concern for any individual student is easily observed to be the first factor sacrificed in the interest of any of various other motivations-in-fact. As with government restricting the rights of each person in the name of protecting the rights of the people, every individual student becomes a dehumanized unit in an implacably-regulated process proclaiming to serve "the individual student."

It is not indictment but observation to say the school system is strongly influenced by such other motivations as these: "*Robotizing*," that is, turning children into employable "worker units" trained to fill certain roles in other industry. Whether seen as socialist horror or as generation-transcending perpetuation of productive order, it is clear no industrial society can long perpetuate itself without instilling in the young the skill, discipline, and reward-motivation which enable them to be used in structured service by industry. This fact supports a certain logic that children are in some measure the property of the industrial state, "raw material" without which it cannot function. It is my personal libertarian opinion that educated free people engaged in professions they honor, proud members of guilds and unions, will not have to be forced to teach their children the ways of honest employment and hard work. Everywhere in history we look, we hate the state which claims to own the worker and his children like cattle or coal, and we call that worker's life "slavery." Likewise, schools in fact perform a certain "*Toilet training*," that is, teaching basic rules of social behavior: punctuality, civility, respect, cleanliness, obedience, conformity, and taboo. Though some might argue these are matters which should be instilled in the home, it is clear our society does not consist only of families who know and practice these principles. If, however, in the name of these behavioral concerns, the schools in actual practice impose the same safety and security modalities used in correctional institutions, then the basic rules of social behavior the children actually learn will be those of the prison, and not of the voluntarily-cooperative democratic free country we keep telling those school children they are growing up in. Schools are responsible for keeping employable youth out of the labor market, yet off the streets, that is, for "*Warehousing*" them. Without such protective incarceration, adolescents would probably be a far more visible part of society as they work out the issues that naturally matter to them: self-discovery, pecking order, sexual stature, and the formation of protective alliances. Whether correctly or not, the school system rigidly inhibits all of these motivations. There is another consideration that has nothing to do with the children at all. That is the school system's role as an organ of "working welfare"in which a huge number of people are employed at public expense serving the children as a social-services *Client group*. Like the prison system, the schools employ large numbers of people whose jobs and mortgaged lives depend on maintaining the status quo. Having identified school children as a client group, the government does not limit services to education, and the children become clients of other agencies also. Their well-being becomes motivation for further expansion of government power, more government jobs, and greater revenue flows. Among such programs are vaccinations, prescriptions, and other medical services (for refusing which, parents can lose children to other state agencies), and the ever-more-efficacious "drug interdiction services" by which "suspiciously-profiled" students come to the helpful attention of various counselors and other inquisitive persons acting for the good of the children in the name of The Senate and The People of Home.

The Lessons Learned

Years will pass before we reap fully the draconian horrors of Zero Tolerance policies in our schools, and in the workplace, and in our neighborhoods. We are all to be the victims of the tragic hypocrisy of using "safety" issues to justify the creation of a penal environment, in and out of school. With the liberals waving their crying towels and building the welfare state, and the conservatives wagging their fingers and building the police state, we have progressed into national socialism to the point where citizens who wave the Constitution are called radicals. Some of our national Zero Tolerance policies were originated by the highly-celebrated head of Las Vegas' school-safety program, a man who studied Police Science in order to play ball in college. If you take your problem to an architect, he will design a building. If you take it to a doctor, he will prescribe drugs. It should come as no surprise then that his solution is to run schools like prisons where students are taught to "play ball" within the system. As it is in prison, student discipline is a summary procedure administered through a labyrinth of official forms and authorizations. Schools are locked down at the bell, and the use of armed officers with metal detectors as campus guards is ubiquitous. A First Amendment exception forbids obscene speech to campus police, who are authorized to arrest offending students, and to submit them to body-cavity search for drugs, weapons, and other possible violations of the safety of the other students and the officers.

The Original Sin was a McGuffin—that is, it doesn't matter what the offense was, the sin was the willful disobedience. That is precisely the problem with Zero Tolerance, and with those who believe in it religiously. It soon no longer matters to ZT Enforcers whether the law is just or sensible. To have chosen to disobey at all is crime enough to deserve punishment. To guarantee that no student will risk anyone's safety by doing any forbidden thing, their solution is to make disobedience impossible. Disobedience to laws against self-abuse is detected in our schools and on our jobs by demanding the contents of our urinary bladders. Such Zero Tolerance for disobedience is totalitarianism at the molecular level.

What can the highly-credentialed, long-experienced (and no-doubt well-wishing) authors of our school policies possibly think students actually believe about the "fundamental American rights" they must acknowledge to pass government class? Do they think because the ZT policy forbidding nudity in films shown on campus bans "Schindler's List" from study in German class that the students had not seen it? Even a cursory objective examination of the literature they like (those violent bands and films you've been warned to fear) reveals readily that our youth are under no illusion about the fact that the practices of public school administration—and adult social regulation—are much like those of Himmler and Beria, the writings of Orwell and Kafka, or films like "Brasil" and "The Matrix".

It apparently eludes the entire power structure of our national school system that if you operate schools like prisons, it does not matter what is taught in the classroom. The lessons learned will be the lessons of life in the joint. Those are clearly observable. Two categories of people live and work there: agents of the State, and the population. To the population, the State is the oppressor, the enemy. To the statist, the population are immoral criminals who must be controlled for their own protection. If one is to have any privacy, it must be sneaked. To survive the coercion of the inmates, one must learn to say nothing, or lie. To survive the coercion of the administration, one must learn to snitch, that is, to tell on other inmates (which betrayal is a major motive for murder). To survive at all, one must belong to "an organized mutually-protective group"—which are almost always racial. Whether dealing with other cons or the keepers, the bottom line is violence—the fist, boot, club, knife, and gun. You sneak, snitch, lie, join a gang, hate authority, and submit or dominate through force—these are the lessons of survival under penal occupation. No one raised in such an environment can possibly be expected to become a successful part of a functioning democracy governing responsibly free citizens. Students "educated" in such an environment must ultimately make a choice between the only two options approved by the architects of the Penal State. Each must become one of the guards, or one of the cons—Good Nazis In Office, Good Niggers In Jail. Anyone who thinks that means goose-stepping Aryans or African-Americans has missed the point.

New Emperor; Same Old Clothes

One of my heroes has always been the little girl who pointed to the naked Emperor and said, "Look, he is wearing no clothes." In years of trying to emulate her, I have learned that the last chapter of the story has always been left off. Though it hasn't been so badly excised of its hard moral lesson as the Disney version of The Little Mermaid, the real story picks up where Little Lily is standing beside her parents watching The Emperor come parading down the street with all His Majesty's Ministers mincing magnanimously along behind. Being a simple child, and without guile, though possessed of at least average intelligence, she found it quite astonishing to see them all waving to the crowds of people, smiling and graciously accepting their applause. How much more astonishing to see her parents likewise smiling in adulation, and waving their patriotic placards proudly proclaiming, "I'd Vote For The Emp!"

"Look Little Lily," the little lady's lovely mother laughed, "here comes The Emperor! Isn't he impressive? Isn't he grand? Can't you tell how important he is? And look at his lovely clothes. Now tell me the truth, child, and don't you dare give me a foolish answer, aren't those the most beautiful clothes you have ever seen in your life?"

Little Lily looked and looked, and she could feel her parents looking very hard at her, and she could feel the hard glare from every Minister's eyes, and from her neighbors' hostile hooded eyes, and from the eyeless eyeglass gaze of the Emperor's Imperial Behavioral Conformance Assistance Officers. She was very much afraid that she might make a mistake, and she didn't want to do that, so she took a big brave breath, and said, "But Mother, look, he is wearing no clothes at all." Everyone gasped, smiles frozen on their faces, eyes wide as chickens waiting for the fox to pounce. "Oh come on," she plunged on precipitously, "look how fat he is, and what a funny little weenie he has."

Like lightning Little Lily's father slapped her smartly across the cheek. "Don't you ever say anything like that again!" he commanded. "Nobody is going to say a daughter of mine is a fool."

Little Lily's mother grabbed her girl away from her frothing father and put hands over her innocent eyes. "She must have some kind of disability," the pleading parent protested piteously. "She must be protected from believing she is seeing such things. Where is the Minister of Social Salvation?"

The Minister of Public Truth came huffing over, and hustling behind him came the Minister of Youth Elementary Enlightenment, and the Minister of Majestic Media. These monitors of the manufactured reality of the otherwise-mindless millions spoke as one, saying, "She speaks slanderous statements about His Majesty. To stabilize safety of society's state of mind, she must be silenced."

The Minister Most Martial marched over with his minions, manfully manifesting military might, and muttered through his megaphone, "She is causing a public disturbance with this subversive outburst, and must be arrested."

The Minister of Bishops, Blessed Babananda of the Baptized Blind Believers, walked across the goldfish pond and said, "Come now, confess. Don't you know it is a sin to call The Emperor a liar?"

"Wait!" cried The Minister of Wardrobe, knowing he was first in line for the hatchet-job attention of the Minister of Capital Relocation. "This only proves The Emperor's Royal Tailors are correct. Only a genuine fool would speak treason and blasphemy in the presence of His Majesty."

"Yes," agreed The Ministers of Mental Hygiene, Civility and Sanity, Humility and Humanity, "presumably her pre-pubescent preoccupation with His Primacy's prodigious pudenda is proof-patent probability of paternal hokey-pokey. How else could she have known what to say she was imagining she saw? If the father is not also a fool, he will submit her to appropriate therapy, and seek counseling."

The masses assembled began to mutter, to mumble, and to moo. Then a voice cried out, and then another, to bleat and bray, "Take her away! Take her away!" Little Lily's parents, pious, patriotic, and patiently pragmatic, presently agreed The Emperor and all his Ministers could not possibly be wrong, so they permitted them to lock up Little Lily for a lot of observation, to give her a good enema and a prescription for tranquilizers, and to send her back home. It is said she stayed in her room and never spoke another word, that is, until The Emperor announced the opening of his new school, a new hospital, and a new park, while she could see construction had begun only on the new Security Residence for Fools. But that is another story.

"Father Washington, Save Us From SEX!"

I have high regards for the good sheep of our communities, and for those who would be their good shepherds, but I know the nature of sheep is to be easily frightened, and to feel safe only in a secure fold guarded by a strong shepherd. Having been around the block a few times, however, I know also that not all the good guys are sheep, much as the shepherds would like to corral and shear us too. If the world of sheep is built of limitation and security, then the world of the goat is built of opportunity and risk. Given our Bill of Rights, America is a good place for both. However, if the taboos and fears of the sheep are imposed on all by force of law, it gets to be a pretty hard place to be a goat…or an eagle, or a unicorn, or anything else.

In the First Amendment to the Constitution, and in many of their other writings, the group of radical freedomists we call Our Founding Fathers made clear their intention that matters of religious doctrine and moral conscience should be made neither the subject of nor the justification for control by government. In blatant violation of that intention, the Christian Coalition has become a sectarian cabal within our government, in complete possession of the electoral power of one major party and the most publicized third party. Proclaiming themselves defenders of public morality, they are constructing a machine of statist power that would make Hitler, Stalin, and Mao drool with envy. They presume that certain things are so destructive to their religion's definitions of personal morality that all citizens must be denied the right to make up their own minds about them, and that the bodies and souls of the citizens are somehow the property of the state, to be protected from physical or moral self-abuse. From these fundamental presumptions depend all of the "blue laws" which have long justified media regulation, personal surveillance, and omnipresent combat-armed law enforcement to control all aspects of the citizens life—these are the prohibition of gambling, alcohol and drugs, suicide, and (the horror of horrors) sex, seeing sex, educating about sex, selling sex, having forbidden sex, showing pictures of sex, even writing words about sex.

Censorship for "protection" against obscenity is the basic foot-in-the-door law which slides those presumptions past the gullible good sheep. If people will believe that seeing pictures of genitals is morally damaging to the observer (or to the immaculate innocence and sanity of his children), they can be persuaded all too easily that government should protect all the people by controlling the communication media to make it impossible for such pictures to be seen. Censorship is the most basic state violation of First Amendment rights. If it is agreed they may take power over our communications to protect us from dangerous information, then they may control anything the sheep can be made to fear. Government would like laws to control the Internet, and their first level of justification is protection against "pornography," as being something dangerous to children and motivational to predatory perverts. There is a certain clear sense in the prohibition of yelling "Fire!" in a crowded theater, but it is a long leap of presumption to use the same logic to prohibit yelling "Fuck!" It is an easy step thereafter, however, to the prohibition of publishing, to the prohibition of private performance, and thus to building the state organs of surveillance and enforcement "necessary" to observe and prevent personal private practice of… well, of anything they decide it is their responsibility to prohibit.

Promoters of censorship justify banning sexual literature as dangerous to society, because it allegedly can motivate disturbed individuals to depraved acts against helpless victims. It may be true—and maybe other psychotics are motivated by old brown shoes, or Shirley Temple movies. If we take the possibility of inducing violence in the reader as justification for banning books, we enter upon very shaky ground. Of all the art and literature in the history of the world, surely none can compare in having motivated more readers to unreasoned violence, injustice, inquisition, hangings, burnings, genocides, and long-ongoing wars, to that trio of quarreling cousins, The Koran, The Torah, and The Bible. If looking at pictures of naked women makes some twisted individual want to kill one, he is certainly not typical of the readership. If we must take his peculiar reaction as just cause for banning all pictures of naked women, then how could we not take the homicidal reactions of those legions of crusaders and avenging angels as justification for banning all three of those contentious occult scriptures? To Hell with The Constitution, let's BAN THE BIBLE to SAVE AMERICA!

Just say "NO!"
...to Smut-Busters.

Obscenity is in the eye of the beholder. Some people cannot tolerate even to think certain things, so they try to ban all which stimulates forbidden images in their minds. Unmoved that the acts they hate may be considered desirable by others, they can not acknowledge that each individual's reaction to any stimulus is his own. Blaming the publisher of words or pictures which distress them, they cry for law enforcement to protect them from their own feelings. A person who cannot confront his own reactions perhaps should be committed to some Institution for the Incompetent. Those who would impose public censorship to protect themselves from seeing things that uncontrollably upset them would make such an institution of the entire community, and would commit us all into it. What is worse, they would have those compelling reactions determine what should be forbidden to all of us inmates for our own good.

We solve no social problems by ordering police to force them out of sight. The very concept of "forbidden subjects of communication" is an invitation to social horror. That any abridging of Constitutional freedom should be granted to restrict publication because of "obscenity" is downright obscene. The obscenity censors' moralist position is strangely inverted. XX-rated stuff is mostly just about people having sex and enjoying it. However, in PG and R, sexual vulnerability and temptation enhance scenes of horror, pain, extortion, and murder. The women of prime-time TV-soaps wield sexual power like a chainsaw, and viewers cheer their cruelty with moral self-indulgence because the producers don't show them taking off their panties for the guest stars. By the curious standards of "obscenity" censorship, people who enjoy erotic subjects are lascivious perverts from whom the community must be protected, and those most disgusted by sex the most moral and sane. Furthermore, they believe their own self-righteous revulsion should be the standard to which the whole community is held.

Censorship abridges the right of the citizen to inform or amuse himself, restricts the right of parents to determine the moral upbringing of their children, usurps the power of the school board to select curriculum, and abrogates the power of the free market to determine which products are traded. Some attempt to justify censorship saying "community standards" demand it. It is never true. Given a free market, community behavior will reflect its actual standards, for better or for worse. If a community's standards-in-fact do not admit of some product, availability of a truckload of it would not lead the community to buy it. When some faction seeks to arm itself with the power of law enforcement to suppress a willing market, its cries of community standards are specious. Moreover, enforcing a show of officially-moral behavior creates the cruel hypocrisy of people stealing forbidden cookies with their left hands, while with their right hands they arrest their neighbors for the same. Suppression of a willing market produces a criminal underground—which is taken as justification for further persecution, which is taken by the oppressed as grounds for active dissent. These are not socially beneficial results.

The central issue is whether adults can be trusted with the right to make their own decisions about what they see, hear, read, show, say, and print. Pro-censorship religious moralists say where sex is concerned, we cannot be trusted, and the power of law enforcement must impose correct standards—that is, the proclaimed standards of their sect. The sanctimonious and self-righteous presumption that one has a moral obligation to take command of another's life if he will not conform to one's own taboos is bigotry enough in the individual. Given power to impose behavior by force of law, it quickly engenders the most intolerant tyranny, wherein dissent is evidence of moral weakness, and disobedience a fundamental sin. The typical obscenity ordinance serves principally to define what is obscene. Most define anything which is (even imagined to be) erotic to be obscene, and any sharing of offending words or pictures to be illicit traffic. Write a sexy love poem, take a snapshot of a naked friend (or God help you, your 8-year-old playing in the family pool), and let someone else see either—and you could be convicted of "pandering obscenity" and fined and imprisoned. Given the freedom, I might like looking at pictures of naked people. I might even get naked with friends and take pictures. Shucks, we might even sell copies. If moralists whose pious concern for my soul leads them to judge any such behavior forbidden sin are able to make it prohibited by enforceable law, then I would be stuck with a choice: let officers of the Agency for Righteousness and Morality (ARM) inspect my home and my life, and cleanse those of whatever offends them, or draw my curtains and join yet another criminal self-abusers' underground.

"Save us, Dub, from Bubba's sins."

Finally a pro-freedom move from Clinton: 130 pardons, but not fairly Presidential, merely personal pardons. Libertarian Harry Browne swore to pardon all drug-users, and cleanse corruption from office. Bubba Razorback pardoned his own family cokehead, his felonious business partners, and those in his camp who violated their offices for his gain, again proving himself the consummate swine. Promoting Ashcroft for AG, Bush II clearly intends from the start to promulgate the agenda of the Christian cabal which installed him. Today, more than ever before, we risk losing our rights, but not for being black, women, or gay. We all stand to lose. Most seem not even to see it coming, yelling "Hallelujah" while the doors close right before their eyes, because it is done in the name of morality, of protecting our daughters from lust, and our sons from iniquity. In free society, it is difficult to keep young Christians from seeing the world presents reasonable and successful social and spiritual alternatives to Christianity at every turn. To those who place their faith in some other name of God, or live by any other orientation, the effect of enforcement of Christian codes is as intrusive and oppressive as the Nazis, Rome under Caesars and Popes, or the ant-hill state of Maoist China.

"Lead us not into temptation," will be taken as political mandate by the regime of Jesus Christ, American, President by proxy, Lord and Fuhrer of the Righteous Rightist Revolution. Wherever the fundamentalist right gains political power, they use the law to see young Christians suffer not the temptation offered by Satan's alternative lifestyles. From tits on TV to Tsiolkovsky, from Charles Darwin to Gary Gygax, they scourge all they touch to save Christians from temptation to make a wrong choice. These are not weekend-Jesus-club Christians. They are consecrated activists, blind-faith fanatics, taught to respect a death of martyrdom, prepared to lay down their lives or take yours, and to vote as they are told is for Jesus sake, swayed by no reason, evidence, or emotion from their evangelical purpose. "Whatever peace man has on earth is won only through waging unending war against sin," they declare. "Only by persevering in that holy *war is peace* to be maintained." They call those who would be saved to submit themselves eternally, to "take the awl in the ear", a sign which identified a slave in Jesus' time. By their own declaration, Christian *freedom is slavery*. They call for the faithful to "know only Christ, and Him crucified", and declare secular knowledge to be Satan's lies, created to weaken their faith. To a believer in that doctrine, *ignorance is strength.* They call for each of God's servants to be his brother's keeper, and to watch his every move for signs of error. In Christian society, *every brother is watching you.* The exhortation to "love thy neighbor, and forgive thy brother,"is purged of liberal misinterpretation by the pious declaration, "A commie homo witch is not my neighbor, he is an evil invader. My brothers are the Jesus-saved Sons of God, not the Goddamned self-serving sons of Satan who won't sell everything to buy into the sacrifice of blood the Bible said Jesus said Moses said Abraham said God said is the One Way we get off the hook for whatever it was Satan talked Eve into talking Adam into doing."

Christianity is not a democratic social structure. It is fundamentally a monarchy, absolute dictatorship of a totalitarian God, by whose authority believers are obligated to live under and to enforce an inflexible law not subject to evidence or reason. Their government on earth will be a totalitarian government. If any group other than Christians (Scientologists or Sunni, for example) were making full use of the media and the courts to promote the wholesale dismantling of the democratic process by stacking the seats of power with their own fanatical agents, and overtly declaring their intentions to replace Constitutional American freedoms with their own oppressive moralistic doctrines, they would be declared treasonous, and the SWAT teams would be sent out to neutralize them. Those who wish for and take action to gain such power as to make the laws of the United States conform to the higher authority of the dogma of their cult, in so doing rendering the Constitution irrelevant, the Congress impotent, and law-enforcement a sectarian tool, are in fact conspiring to overthrow the government of the United States. A President who elevates to power a person whom he knows will interpret or change the Constitution so as to make it conform to the Bible or any other religious, occult, or philosophical creed is in violation of his oath to support and defend the Constitution, and is in fact an active member of that conspiracy. Is that not an impeachable offense?

Freedom Is Our
Community Standard

We do not solve our social problems by ordering our police to keep them out of sight, but rather by open, honest, and tolerant examination of the truth in all our activities. The very concept of "forbidden communication of knowledge" seems to me an invitation to social horror. What a strange and backward attitude the erotic-censors' seems to me, their moralist position strangely inverted. The sexual violence they claim to be caused by "pornography" is not found in the X-rated stuff, which is pictures of people having sex and enjoying it. However, in the PG and R films, sexual vulnerability and temptation are used to enhance scenes of horror, pain, extortion, power manipulation, murder, and dismemberment. The women of prime-time TV soaps wield sexual power like a chainsaw, and viewers cheer their cruelty with moral self-indulgence because the producers refrain from showing the scenes where they take off their panties with the guest stars. It is not that pornography will engender sexual violence that moralists fear, but that forbidden acts might appear pleasant. By their standards, those who enjoy freedom of knowledge of erotic subjects are branded lascivious perverts, sickos from whom the community must be protected, while those whose reactions are disgust and loathing declare themselves most moral and sane. Insisting their self-righteous revulsion should be the standard by which the whole community is measured, promulgators of obscenity censorship demand the power of law enforcement to deny to all whatever offends their personal emotions and tastes.

If such a law is permitted in a community, what will prevent the overzealous from amending it to prohibit that which they find offensive for heresy, blasphemy, political subversiveness, ethnic sensitivity, or disrespect to sacred symbols and figures of authority in church and state? God save us from "public servants" who believe they must protect our children from their own visions of evil by using social shame, enforced ignorance, and criminal status to build stronger and higher walls around their minds…and ours. Some people cannot tolerate even to think certain things, so they try to ban anything which stimulates forbidden images in their minds. Unmoved that the acts they abhor may be harmless, voluntary, even considered desirable by others, they can not acknowledge that each individual's reaction to any stimulus is uniquely his own. Blaming the publisher of the words or pictures, they cry for the power of law enforcement to protect them from their own feelings. From one point of view, a person who cannot control his own reactions ought to be committed to institutional care for incompetence. Those who would impose public censorship to protect themselves from seeing things that upset them would make such an institution of the entire community, and would commit us all into it. What is worse, they would have themselves (that is, their uncontrollable reactions) be the judges of what should be forbidden to all of us inmates for our own good.

The obscenity ordinances some are trying to propose for our communities would specifically authorize the use of armed police to confiscate from our shops any literature deemed prurient, that is, pertaining to or showing anything sexual, and to take those books and tapes out and destroy them. Have we forgotten those piles of books burning in the streets of 1930's Berlin for the crime of pertaining to anything pro-Jewish? There is no easier way to create a sick and oppressive society than by declaring common human qualities to be evil and therefore illegal. The typical obscenity ordinance (usually based on Miller vs. California) serves principally to define in legal terms what is obscene. Specifically, it defines all that which is erotically explicit to be obscene. Further, it would impose the ban of censorship on all such material by forbidding the "promotion" of it by: "manufacture, issue, sell, rent, give, provide, advertise, lend, mail, deliver, transfer, transmit, publish, distribute, circulate, disseminate, present, display, exhibit, or to offer or agree to do the same." Should you write an erotic love poem, or take a snapshot of a naked friend, and offer to let someone else see either, you could by the letter of such an ordinance be convicted of "pandering obscenity", and fined and imprisoned. The central issue in censorship is whether or not adults in a free country can be trusted with the right to make their own decisions. Pro-censorship's position says where sex is concerned, we cannot be trusted, and the power of law enforcement must be applied to impose correct standards—that is, the prohibitionists' own. The reasoning: given choice, we make wrong moral judgements, proving ourselves too weak to exercise freedom. In compassion, they must therefore assume the burden of usurping our Constitutional right of individual citizen's power and exercising it on our behalf to control our unrighteous urges.

Given freedom, I might look at erotic pictures of naked people. I might get naked with friends and take pictures. Heck, we might even sell copies. Moralist authoritarians assert such acts are evil and obscene, and they take that as a mandate to impose control by civil force upon my untrustworthy abuse of my freedom. If they succeed in making that which is erotic illegal by calling it obscene, I will have a choice: let them cleanse my home of whatever offends them, or draw my curtains and become part of a brand new criminal underground. The sanctimonious and self-righteous idea that one has a moral obligation to take command of another's life if he will not conform to one's own taboos is bad enough in the individual. When it is given the power to impose behavior with the force of law, it quickly engenders the most intolerant tyranny, wherein dissent is evidence of moral weakness, and disobedience of the law is a fundamental sin. It is evil's most insidious trick that one who would defend freedom must appear to defend evil. For one group of people to forcibly usurp the freedom of choice of another group is evil, even if done with the best of faith in their own righteousness, and in full compliance with the process of law.

I believe the Fathers of our Constitution were wise to guarantee that certain rights shall not be abridged, by law or in fact. Such freedom demands that standards of morality must be maintained by some means other than the power of civil law enforcement. It must come from the community, not as a cry for government to exercise more power by law, but as a collective act of establishing the community's standards in fact. Merely electing the rulers who command the police is a poor excuse for democracy.

We who oppose the so-called "anti-obscenity" laws do not seek to promote obscenity, though our detractors are quick to accuse us of just that. I should like to believe no citizen calling for such an ordinance wishes to destroy the basic rights which make our way of government the most just in history. I can acknowledge those socially-conscious citizens are attempting in good faith to define the "responsible" part of "responsible freedom", whereas we are attempting to defend the "freedom" part. The point of contention is the use of enforced prohibitionary law. If one group would ban obscenity, and the other would ban tyranny, then clearly the resolution must come from tolerance and respect of each other's rights and desires. We must all act upon the common goal of preserving both our communities' high moral standards and also our country's precious guarantees of freedom.

Some sects' morality exhorts abstention from certain acts which others might call normal sexual behavior. The penitent may voluntarily choose to accept such limitations as a sacrifice made in faith, and they violate the rights of no one. However, when moralists insist that to avoid temptation for such penitents to violate their vows, everyone else must be forced to behave as though we were also abstemious penitents, then they violate the rights of all, and invalidate the faith of the penitent.

Censorship would abridge the right of the citizen to inform or amuse himself, would restrict the right of parents to determine the moral upbringing of their children, would usurp the power of the school board to select the curriculum, and abrogate the power of the free market to determine which products are desired and which are spurned. By creating resentment, it would even undermine the power of the churches to create high moral standards through inspiration. And that is where our moral standards should come from, not from enforcement, but through inspiration, example, encouragement, and active participation of the citizen in the affairs of the community.

Some attempt to justify censorship with the declaration that community standards demand it. If that were true, availability of obscene material by the truckload would not lead the community to buy it. When one faction feels it must arm itself with the power of law enforcement to suppress a willing market among others, then cries of "community standards" are specious. Those who would impose some bizarre, paranoid, and oppressive obscenity ordinance are not reacting to community standards. They are attempting to dictate standards, and to impose them by force. I find that obscene.

Given a free market for ideas, community behavior will reflect the true standards of the community, for better or for worse. Enforcing an unwilling show of officially-moral behavior can only result in the cruel hypocrisy of a society in which people steal forbidden cookies with their left hands, while with their right hands they arrest their neighbors for the same. Suppression of a willing market among those who would be free produces a criminal underground, which is taken by the suppressors as justification for further persecution, which is taken by the suppressed as grounds for active social dissent, which justifies the riot squads… and history wonders why we were shooting at each other over pictures of naked people.

No Christmas
in Town Hall?

I like Christmas, notwithstanding I do not subscribe to Christian theology or doctrine. I agree with the First Amendment that precludes making any law which would "respect" an establishment of religion. Adding my mote to the opinions of hundreds more learned, I interpret that to mean no law may be passed which grants official endorsement to any doctrine or dogma as being equivalent to empirical science, which grants favor before the law to any religious body, or which employs law enforcement to impose the taboos or sacraments of any particular sect. It would seem clear any reasonable interpretation would render thousands of laws now enforced in every state unquestionably unconstitutional. To begin with, consider laws which define what is and is not an establishment of religion. If any established congregation is, to use the new PC term, "faith-based," then it is the faith of the faithful which makes it a religious body, and not a decision made by any board of legislators. If government has no authority to define and so limit by law that which is an establishment of religion, so as to deny unqualified establishments, there is not even reason to keep an official government registry of them. Though any group of faithful are certainly free to call themselves a congregation and conduct their rituals in public or in secret, it is only by registry and licensing by government that such a group becomes an "establishment" of any kind. Why should any religious organization wish to permit (or even encourage) the government to make any unconstitutional laws respecting them? Even a cursory look at the most common laws respecting religious establishments as different from other establishments makes the answer all too tragically simple: power and money. The most obvious is of course the exemption from paying taxes that other establishments must submit to. Others include "blue laws" imposing restrictions on property owners and businesses respecting their proximity to religious establishments or schedule of ritual. Since the first Vestry with the most members in office agreed to permit Legislature the power to define and license religious establishments in return for that fiduciary respect, the Church has been whoring its constituency to the State for public money and law enforcement. This relationship is proclaimed illicit by both Constitution and Scripture, for reasons clear to anyone who appreciates Constitutional freedom from government, or who celebrates personal communion of the individual soul with the eternal spirit without imposition of an idolatrous authoritarian chain of communication and command.

Unfortunately, the most vocal of the opponents of this meretriciousness have taken the stand that the government must therefore purge itself of all that might be seen as supporting one or another religion...any religion. Wrong! Read the Amendment: "Congress shall make no law respecting an establishment of religion, or prohibiting the free exercise thereof...." We seem to have forgotten that second part. We have a majority of one religion in America, and that one is openly seeking to use its plurality to obtain high office and thereby impose its notions of morality and truth by enforced law. Others call for the power of government to be exercised to remove from any "public" place any display of the symbols or celebrations of that particularly predatory sect, and all others as well. Both seek greater government license to pass laws respecting that establishment of religion, one for it, the other against. Both have missed the point. The point of religious freedom without respect for any establishment is that all religious activity may flourish without any sect seizing secular power, and without anyone being prevented by government forces from openly celebrating his faith, especially on public property. Though I decry and rebuke the sectarian cabal which so proudly and publically wears its robes in the halls of Congress, I must still object to prohibition of their colors. No Christmas in Town Hall? Didn't that line up there say, "no law....prohibiting the free exercise thereof"? Run the carolers off the Court House steps with riot control troopers? Tear down the World War I memorial in Idaho because it is cross-shaped? Valgame Dios! God forbid that should come to pass in America. Which means, of course, that we must be as willing to accommodate other public celebrants who are well enough established to put on a good show. The Mary and Joseph thing is a joy to watch, no matter how seriously you take their offspring's reputation. I'll take all that kind of stuff I can get, whether it's about Winnie the Witch, Mahmoud the Muslim, Deirdre the Druid, Hassan the Sufi, Buddha-Belly Baba, Benji the Buddhist (and Benji the Bahai), Norman the Mormon, Jersey Jerzy Jew, Ziggy Zen, Harry Krishna, Ozzie Osiris, Thuper Thor, or Hey-Zeus. The God I know is big enough for all of them. Merry Christmas!

Is Halloween Satanic?

Once upon a time there was a beautiful religion based on respect for nature, on creating safe and loving communities, maintaining health by knowing nature's ways and remedies, and worshiping the eternal spirit through ritual celebrations of fertility and the holy cycle of life. They call their religion Wicca, from which we get the words "wise" and "witch". Wiccans did not believe mankind was evil, or born in debt to God, or had to shed anybody's blood to please God and keep from Hell. Therefore, they did not wish to join the cult of guilt, fear, and sacrifice which swept their land with armed priests, and flaming stakes. They refused to bow down to the idol that cult had made of a martyred Jewish prophet. For refusing their divinely-ordained yoke, those militant self-proclaimed agents of God declared Wiccans were worshipers of Satan and deserved the torch, though Wiccans knew Satan is only a mythological character. Wiccans still have a celebration about the same time as Halloween, called Samhain. It is devoted not to Satan, but to the Goddess, for the goodness of plentiful earth. The idea God might be female is heresy by Christian dogma, and those who believed it were hunted down, tried by pious male judges, divested of their estates, and killed. After persecution drove Wiccans into hiding, Christians created a day of "giving the Devil his due," the shtick being to dress up in images of death and evil: corpses, devils, and witches. It is a mockery by which the young are taught that witches are sadistic evil old hunchback women who cook bat soup, consort with the Devil, and presumably eat Christian children. Halloween identifies other such "occult" symbols with Satan as pointed hats and those mysterious evil wraiths called ghosts. (Is St. Jude a ghost? What does necromancy mean?) The truth, of course, is that the only evil in black cats, bats, skeletons, pentagrams, astrological symbols, Hebrew letters, or out-thrust tongues, is the evil the judgmental insist on putting there. Then they self-righteously accuse anyone associated with those images of their own sinister judgements. Christian paranoia and bigotry created the absurd spectacle of Halloween to teach children that certain non-Christians are evil. The symbols used are as far from the truth about witchcraft as the rabbit with the technicolor eggs is from the truth about Christ. The fact that young people stretching the limitations of their elders' conventions choose number 666 or the inverted star as symbols of independence hardly means they become minions of The Infinitely Evil Satan (minor chord; drum roll). If Happy Meals for a pair of Cub Scouts costs $6.66, that does not mean Ronald McDonald or one of the Cubs is the Anti-Christ. Putting a star on his hat would not make your kid a Communist; a star on his shoulder would not make him a General; and even carving one on his forehead would not of itself make him a Satanist.

But no, Christians who fear Satan's insidious influence are not really paranoid. Satan is everywhere, ready to poison their minds. Consider that even our days of the week (taught in public schools from kindergarten) are named for Pagan gods. Sun-day, and Mon(moon)day are straight from Astrology, a superstitious doctrine practiced by Satanists, promiscuous LSD-heads, and weekly-tabloid false prophets. Saturday (Saturn's day) is not only Astrological, it is even named for a false god worshiped by Pontius Pilate's deicidal Roman stormtroopers. Wednesday is Wotan's day, after the deity of bloodthirsty Vikings, as is Thursday (Thor's day), named for his (not His) son. Friday is Frigga's day, taken blatantly from the mythology of Druids and evil witches.

Tuesday is Tiu's day, for the Teutonic god of war, a false deity from the same myths Adolf Hitler believed in when he said Germans were the master race, diabolically giving "White ethnic pride" a very bad name. Satan would like us to keep the names of ancient false gods alive, along with other diabolical notions like evolution, reincarnation, geophysics, herbal medicine, and water-witching. If Evil is not to triumph in America, surely we must stop using our social institutions to promote the opponents of God by at least eliminating the horde of Satan's demigods whose names we are forced to honor weekly. Why can't we name our days in character with our role as a nation under God, a nation so tolerant as to legally harbor every doctrine no matter how false good Christian reasoning reveals it to be. For Monday, let us have Lukes (which will be good for Spanish speakers used to Lunes). For Tuesday, Markes, which mirrors the Spanish Martes. For Wednesday, Matthes, and for Thursday, Johnnes. For Friday, not Thor's mother, but Maryday. Following the Spanish again, Saturday is simply Sabbaday, and Sunday is obviously Sonday. The old days' characters, Thor, Roman, and Hippie Astrologer, will become fearfully-evil Halloween masks.

There Is No Millennium.

The power of the millennium is attributed to being 1000 years after the birth of Jesus. So what was the "date" then? There is no record of it in writings from the time, all dated according to some other calendar. Each calendar traced its origin to some event—the "date" of which is meaningful only if traced from some other event .So "when" did any of it happen, and what makes one time more important than another? Timekeeping through history has been done by observing celestial bodies, a science called astronomy. The notion that any arrangement of planets, or date, has psychological or divine significance is called astrology. Using computers, we can determine the position of planets at any time in history. In the year we call 7 BC, a conjunction—"a sign in the stars"— occurred which would be interpreted by astrologers east of Bethlehem as heralding the birth of a new king in the west. If that astrological interpretation of that astronomical event might be taken as correct dating of the birth of Jesus, then anything intended to happen 2000 years after that happened in 1993. Did we miss the end of the world? Or worse, has it already ended, and is this the hell to which we have been damned?

Extrapolating present trends creates a picture of a hellish world to come. It seems negativistic to point out terrible consequences of steps we are blithely taking, when our lives today are so abundant. In the buffets of Las Vegas, the variety, quantity, and quality of food is unmatched in the world, and in history. In all of human existence, no one has ever eaten better than we do. That is a sobering thought. Even so, a few things seem clear. Though the War On Drugs has been the most destructive influence on Constitutional freedom, civil security, and trust in government in this century, it continues to escalate. It will pale in comparison to the War On Guns. Whereas the first is justified by the presumption that your body is the State's to protect, and its destruction of your life done to protect you from yourself, the War On Guns is presumed to be protecting others from you, so anything goes. Domestic terrorists, after all, have no rights at all. When freedom-loving Americans resist drug laws by smoking dope, nobody gets hurt. But when "2nd Amendment gun-nuts" stand up for their rights by shooting back at storm-troopers who come to get their Vietnam War trophies, the do-do will hit the fan. Even one such incident will initiate an entry-on-demand / no-knock-if-we-want policy, and people will be killed believing they have the right to defend their homes. It will also justify domestic use of all high-tech surveillance and intervention equipment available to the military.

However, the War On Guns is only Act II. Perhaps the year 2000 will be significant after all as the year the War On Sin began. The presumption that your body is property of the State, to be protected with laws against self-abuse is piddling compared to the presumption that your soul is property of the Church, to be protected from the eternal consequences of your sin—by law enforcement. This is not new—all "blue laws" are enforced statutes which forbid acts only because they are moral taboo to the prevailing religion. The fact the Constitution forbids union of Church and State does not deter them. The fact that Scripture refers to a religious body which beds down with civil authority and embraces the deadly sword of law enforcement as a "whore fornicating with the kings of the Earth" does not deter them. This is to be their year of victory, and they are filled with rejoicing in themselves, in God's name. In Cabal, the high-priests of the Coalition speak of "Dominion" as their filial divine responsibility and right, and insofar as they worship a totalitarian idol of God, they will not be satisfied until they command a totalitarian regime in His name. A Christian Ayatollah in the White House will use the power of American might to smite the sinful of the earth—starting at home. What can be done about it? Nothing. Most will vote for it in the year 2000, and still be surprised when they find reason to come for you.

Here are some predictions for the coming year: The End of the World will not happen. California will not fall into the sea. The aliens will not return to Area 51 with Jesus after a thirty-year trip at light-speed. No one will rise up into the sky to the strains of a brass sextet with wings. The computers are not going to crash—The Borg will survive just fine. Cher will marry again, to me.

"Keep It Private, Citizen."

An important freedom is the right to privacy, as intended by the term "private citizen". It is not specifically mentioned in the Constitution, though many of the stipulated rights obviously depend upon it. Though any social activity requires giving up a degree of one's privacy, and most prefer not to be hermits, it should be possible in a free state to live without any official body demanding to know one's location, sex, race, age, extent of personal holdings including home, pockets, or bladder, income including money, trade, or service, or the names of those with whom one does business, has sex, or discusses politics. The demand that automobiles be registered and display the number is a good example of government invasion of privacy disguised as public service. Registration is touted as protecting the citizen from theft. This is illusion, as license plates do not prevent theft, nor much improve the chance of recovery. Even if service were the true objective, it should be voluntary. Even mandatory, it need be done only once, not annually. Clearly, the primary benefit is to enable government to establish identity and observe the movement of the owner. Licensing provides no service to the citizen, but grants higher levels of surveillance and control over him—and he must pay for it! It is argued that fees provide revenue needed to operate the public service system. That is like being interrogated by electroshock to obtain information the State would use to control you, then being charged for the electricity. When it comes to pressing the citizen for details of his life, the Motor Vehicle Department is small time. If, God forbid, it should become a matter of State interest to know where all the Jews live, how many places have records stipulating religious or ethnic denomination? How about that new pan-demographic Census? What about that IRS? Sometime, just for fun, try to convert $20,000 of your resources into $100 bills, carry them to another state by airline, spend the money on firearms and gold, and get the stuff home…without leaving your name on anything.

Here is a little parable to illustrate the problem. "Back In The USSR?"

Two men huddled in a bleak corner of the drab concrete city. Clothes threadbare, they were gaunt men, but they felt lucky to have a small brazier to warm their hands. One drew reflectively on a pipe, though he had nothing to put into it. "Tell me, friend," he said, "why you sit here in the cold with me, who has nothing, when I know you own a fine vehicle. Here there is no food, while crops lie heavy in the rural fields. Surely if you went out and brought back produce, you could become rich. Do not the principles of Capitalism say real economic power lies in private ownership of the means of production?"

The other chuckled wryly. "Yes, free enterprise is the rule. There are just a few minor technicalities. First I must register my vehicle (and pay a fee), get a license to drive, for which I must take an exam on the regulations (instructor's fee), then a driving test in a vehicle that meets regulations—mandatory inspection (mechanic's fee), safety equipment (retailer's fee), and insurance (agent's fee)—after which I may pay the fee to get a business licence. To carry and sell produce, I must have a Health Code inspection (fee), and an environmental impact assessment (fee). To conduct commercial transport, I must pay for a drug-test program on my only employee, myself. To conduct interstate trade, I must pay a bonding fee. Since I have no money, I must borrow on my vehicle to buy produce, and pay interest. When I buy, I pay sales tax. When I sell, I pay receipts tax. Since I have an employee (myself), I pay Social Security and worker's government insurance fees. I pay self-employment tax on everything after expenses, and when I keep what remains, I pay personal income tax on that. What I must pay for government permission, mandatory expenses which increase neither productivity nor value, mandatory insurance, and taxes outweigh what profit might be made in the produce I could carry—that is, without gouging the consumer. And the consumer can only pay so much before he cannot afford to buy at all, whereupon my produce and my capital investment both rot in the vehicle, while the hungry curse me for my greed. For failure to pay them back, my creditors will sieze my vehicle, and for failure to pay their taxes and fees, the government will take whatever else I have. If I tried to obey all the laws, it would ruin me. If I got caught breaking one, they would destroy me. Perhaps someday we will have free enterprise, and success will lie in ownership of the means of production, the entrepreneurial spirit, and the willingness to work. Until then, success depends on paying for government permission, regulation, and protection. Since those belong exclusively to the federal-contract mega-businessmen who own the government, my vehicle might as well be a rock." And nothing ever happened to them, forever and ever after.

You Bet, You Can Bet!

You bet, betting should be permitted on College sports. The players are doing nothing more or less wicked no matter who bets on their game, skims tickets, or sleeps with the coach. Heck, why not bet on the Little League? The temptation to tempt the babes to cheat? Are those who write the do-do-no-no's into law just reacting to their own paranoid image of demonic game-fixers lurking the Middle Schools like happy-pill-peddling pedophiles looking to tempt their innocent lambs with the rewards of learning the subtle skills of point-shaving?

How true is the notion that a free citizen has the right to spend, give away, throw away, or otherwise dispose of whatever property he owns? Do we have ANY property the government may not control if it chooses to? I think not. It would make criminals of those who risk our personal property on the outcome of a ballgame, or the roll of dice. Everyone who enters a game knows not everybody wins, and nobody wins all the time (except maybe those who haven't heard cigarettes hurt them (or school kids used to races where everyone gets a ribbon, so nobody goes home a loser)). That is why casinos call it a game, instead of something sneaky like "mandatory insurance" ...also a bet, on the outcome of your accident. If betting is legal activity the citizen is free to do, why should the subject of the bet matter? On what grounds might government insist one may spend money on tobacco, but may not bet it on a duck race? If not for the understandable racket called "licensing" (that is, government granting to one citizen a right it denies to others, upon payment of money to the right agency's bagma…I mean, citizen-service revenue-receiving associate) why should not any free citizens agree among themselves upon the terms of any bet? "Hey, buddy, 'betcha two t'one my kid scores before yerz. A hunnert bucks." "Yer on, chumpo."

Where do they come from, all these so-called "blue laws" regulating such personal practices as drinking, drug use, gambling, and prostitution? The generalist term most often used is "moral values." Sometimes given weight as "traditional values," these laws are well-intentioned as protecting the weak-willed from self-destruction. Since ancient cultures in holy books also discouraged certain activities, many presume these prohibitions are "God's laws." Be that as it may, it does not make them law of the land. Making any sectarian taboo a generally enforced law would seem a violation of the Constitution's prohibition of using law enforcement to grant respect to any religion as above all. Each of these laws prohibiting something "moralists" think nobody should make their own choices about depends on certain presumptions. First, that anyone other than the free citizen should use power to make his moral decisions for him, and second, that government should let those decisions be made by legislators to follow any doctrine of religion.

For a well-intentioned busybody to believe he serves his fellow man by law-enforced punishment for disobedience to those closer to God than themselves, is some presumption. To believe he serves God by making his brother a better soul than God made him, is the height of self-righteousness. To believe himself morally superior, favored by his God because he is willing in the name of "protecting his brothers' souls from their sins of vice" to declare them criminals, to persecute, imprison, disenfranchise, impoverish by statutory asset-robbery, to beat, interrogate, "medicate," coerce into dangerous "informant" roles, even to kill them…is, well, if it were being done by anyone other than state-employed followers of the predominant religious sect, it would be called psychopathic by the shrinks and lawyers, and Satanic by you-know-who. Such a person, well-intentioned as he may be, presumes that the bodies, and even the souls of those brothers somehow belong to him, that he as God's steward should take upon himself to protect them from the moral errors of those to whom God so unwisely gave them.

No self-styled moralist has any right to prohibit gambling by others. That fact doesn't change the law or the reality. If it were no longer prohibited, free citizens might decide to bet on all kinds of things. The "powers that be" would organize and collect the vig, but they would for sure open the games up, not put some tight-shoe schoolmarm squeeze on us for our own good. Could be a lot of fun. Why, fer example, should we not bet on politics? Offer a spread on electoral votes: Bush -34, flat; Browne +42, Gore... who cares. Who's got a line on Libertarian Carla Howell vs. Ted Kennedy? 125 to 1? I saw the Rams at that last year, didn't I?

Only Crooks Use Cash.

Only criminals use lots of cash, right? To stop the drugs, guns, and bet runners, follow the cash. Would there be no crime if we outlawed cash, and switched to universal card accounts, which like your VISA know what you purchased, where, and when? If using a card means identifying yourself and your location, then no one wanted for anything could use it. Far from eliminating all the criminals, this would force people into the underground who were leading productive even if furtive lives. This is not unlike government giving welfare to unwed mothers if they name the "deadbeat dad" failing to provide, making him unemployable, of necessity a criminal. To say total accounting of everyone's transactions may fairly be called "free enterprise" is like saying there is freedom in prison to obey the rules. It "levels the field" by prostrating all. If government can rule what you may possess, which of your assets you may trade, the price, and how much you must pay for the privilege of trading (as it does today), then the only free enterprise is underground. Only there can two citizens agree upon the worth of their assets and exchange them freely, without a government agent in the middle dictating the terms of the deal, for a forced fee. The Drugwar is promulgated in spite of clear evidence it causes more damage than drugs do, because (among other reasons) it entitles government surveillance and control over our personal transactions, and global transactions. It is war on privacy of person, privacy of possession, and privacy of transaction. The Devil's Dope is just the football, but the game is control of your life and money. If any agency had power to know, permit or deny every transaction, then everything would belong to it in practice, to do with as its policy dictated. Elimination of private exchange in favor of a "crime-proof" FEDCARD Agency would make its officers the rulers of the world, and create a huge, hostile, and resourceful underground.

The FEDBANK Empire opens with the key that says TAX. If the card is used to collect tax, then government may control how it treats its account holders. If taxation continues to be item-specific, and region-specific, then every product and service will require an identifier, a location code, tax rate, and official fair market value. The resulting World Blue Book would be a global price-fixing tool. It would have thousands of authorized terminals constantly updating some category or other, the consequences of new legislation, or recalculation of some index. The ability to access the database for marketing would be more valuable than blood, and black-market FEDCARD data might become a medium of illicit exchange at a certain level of society. The power to control the master program is to drink from the Holy Grail while wearing the Ring of the Niebelung, wrapped in Superman's cape. The opportunity to trade an important oil evaluation fix for a crop of cocaine to distribute for the swing vote of a demographic group might make a kingpin of Colombia's elected and trusted delegate to the Board of Trustees, and not leave a track for the bean-counter robots to follow. The door slams shut with the lock that says LAW. Once in place for taxation, its potential takes totalitarianism to draconian new levels. Gum is illegal in Singapore, raw eggs in California. The gun you bought at Sears last year is illegal now and must be surrendered. That book has been declared obscene by City Ordinance 264-A1, and cash registers in this town won't sell it. Everything has a legal category, and every person's category would be checked with every purchase. Felon? Can't buy a gun. DWI? Can't buy beer. Driver's license expired? Can't buy gasoline. Business license expired? The Master Control Program will not permit deposits to your account. People do not stop eating when their bank account is closed by aparatchiks or subroutine 264-D. The "unaccountables" find some way to survive. Barter media are spontaneously created, and like the regulated counterpart the stock market, are faddish in valuation. Lots of things become media for illegal or other cashless trade, as hippies used beadwork, hash-pipes, and the like to take the place of dollars which demanded somebody get straight jobs. Was a time when cocaine dealers used Indian jewelry to avoid carrying cash. You might expect something like baseball cards, CD records maybe, but with rare ones known to be more valuable. "A '92 Madonna? Give ya fifty... tell ya what, sixty gallons, FED-clean, no record, my brother."

Cross-breed the cell phone, global locator, driver's license, and your bank card, and you've got the USACARD. When you hold it (or implant it), its built-in skin-resistivity meter (that's a lie detector) tells the USA how you feel about the questions it asks, and you don't even have to answer. Hey, that'll stop crime for sure, and then we can enjoy a little peace and freedom around here.

The Green Police

Citizen activists of Elko NV's Jarbridge Rebellion are drawing national attention attempting to prevent The Mighty Fed from closing a popular road to protect endangered trout. The hard fact is, of course, that keeping all human beings out of any area is the only way to keep it wilderness. To permit people to visit is to destroy it, like it or not. Is the only answer to this dilemma to permit government to decide which places the citizen may visit, and which are forbidden zones? Liberal authoritarians are quick to abridge the rights of all to protect the interest of a helpless few. Conservative authoritarians as quickly abridge the rights of all to protect a powerful few. Libertarians proclaim the government should remain hands-off, permitting private owners of land to protect it or develop it as they wish. In practice, government has demonstrated it might choose to force the private conservationist to permit an easement for a public road, or might just as likely forbid the private developer to move one stone if doing so appears to destroy some form of habitat it may happen to identify on his property. Unfortunately, none of these government policies is able to guarantee the survival of any species, nor to guarantee future generations the right to visit the primordial wilderness their grandparents knew.

Here is a bit of speculative "future history" to illustrate my take on the problem.

"Once upon a time, at the insistence of mobilized popular concern for the survival of endangered species and the preservation of the natural environment, well-wishing public servants in government instituted The Green Police. These armed agents of the Department of The Interior were given the responsibility and power to make sure nobody broke any of the laws, statutes, regulations, policies, rulings, or restraining orders protecting the forest and its natural inhabitants. Since motor vehicles, structures, campsites, fires, fuels and toxic substances, firearms, hunting or trapping devices, chainsaws and axes, mining, digging, or dredging equipment, refuse dumping, construction, damming, drainage, et cetera, and etc. were potentially harmful to the forest, or to the natural habitat of some indigenous species, all were made illegal within the EPZ's—that is, the Environmental Protection Zones.

"Being confident they had thus done their part to save the planet and sooth the hearts of their concerned constituents, the legislators retired to the baths with their favorite lobbyists. They were soon disturbed by new outcry from those same environmental activists whose demands they had just fulfilled. Those passionate saviors of nature were calling for something to be done about the sudden increase in the number of criminals who were desecrating the newly-hallowed ground of the EPZ. Not to be gainsaid by insubordinate, lawless, and socially irresponsible commoners, the Officers of State dutifully met the demand by substantially increasing the number of Green Police, and providing them with every modern technological advantage so as to accomplish their sworn duty to the People and the Land. Naturally, costs were very high for their competitive salaries and extensive training, their fine new equipment, and the many new employees needed for their administrative support—not to mention the costs of involving other law-enforcement agencies to protect them from hostile hordes of squatters, poachers, Sunday-coachers, fence-jumpers, scum-dumpers, and other trespassing environmental terrorists. To fund such expensive public service, the Department Of Interior was granted the power to award government contracts to manage certain resources of the EPZ—that is, to conduct the business of limited logging, trapping, mineral development, and (for those with very special permission) tourism. To save the forest, armies of The Green Police patrolled the limits of the legally-habitable areas, while government-sanctioned environmental defense contractors cut down the trees."

Want To Go To Space?
Learn Russian.

Best recent news is that entrepreneurs plan to turn Mir Space Station into a resort, and Russia is eager to let anyone with the money play. Growing up at White Sands, I was thrilled to see my Dad and his friends shoot the last of Hitler's V-2's, and embarrassed to see Sputnik and Gagarin reach orbit first. The greatest tragedy of Challenger was not the loss of seven pioneers, but that the Shuttle did not fly for so long thereafter. The notion we could not continue to accept known risks while lawyers, politicians, and journalists held up development of space whining for guaranteed safety, liability litigation, or politically-motivated investigations is an insult to American pioneering courage. Though test crews since the beginning of flight have lost lives in pursuit of progress, lawyers took advantage of the celebrity of Challenger to press for huge settlements, driving up the cost of insuring everything in the program. Money for space goes not to research, but to insurance companies, to protect the engineers from the lawyers. Our safety record is high, not because lawyers are concerned for the feelings of heirs of the brave, but because our engineers are damn good. The only thing stupider than letting preachers dictate science to school boards is letting lawyers dictate science to engineers. Any one-eyed moron not brainwashed by catechism can tell the religion is fantasy, but since lawyers spend years in school memorizing books of arcane rulings, they can pose as educated, and it is harder to tell they have no clue what reality is.

Whence the notion it is atrocity to permit any American the right to risk life for progress, or amusement? Until Chuck Yeager started hanging it out on his meager Captain's pay, most aeronautical envelope-stretching was done by civilians like Howard Hughes, Wiley Post, and Amelia Earhart, whose only motivation was to go faster, farther, or to do it first. How about a vote of confidence from Americans? Give us a chance to prove our faith in the Shuttle, and we'll pay our way doing it. How about a raffle, a big ballyhoo wherein we may buy a chance at a seat equivalent to Christa McAuliffe's on the next STS? At $25, it wouldn't take many to pay for the payload. Millions every year pay more to watch a ballgame. It could be NASA's most profitable cargo! No matter how practical the money and public interest generated may seem, it is not likely. NASA would instantly be bound in gambling litigation, and insurance would exceed the cost of the payload. Congress would take the money to be accounted, appropriated, and re-disbursed (minus handling charges). Security paranoids would label any assertion the people have a right to use the Shuttle "suspiciously leftist".

Perhaps no issue has greater long-term significance than commercial development of Space. Low Earth Orbit, Geosynchronous Orbit, the LaGrange points, and the Moon comprise the high ground of the 21st Century. Whoever controls those places will inevitably dominate the world, and control will fall to those most able to establish permanent presence and profitable use. In our country's first century, mastery of the sea meant world control. When asked to fund America's first Army airplanes, Calvin Coolidge inquired, "Why not buy one and let the pilots take turns?" General Billy Mitchell was cashiered for declaring his superiors irresponsible for the same short-sightedness. When war compelled the bureaucrats to step aside for the engineers, American air power won World War II, and has been the controlling factor in all things military and commercial since. Letting Russia or Japan or anyone else have controlling presence in space is like being able to build the best ships in the world, but refusing to go to sea.

Most space experts are cool-tempered people with no use for hype or hokum, but Americans in general seem most moved by sports, soap-opera politics, give-away shows, and fantasy epic adventures. NASA's best public advocate was probably Gene Roddenberry, whether or not they knew it. American space development can succeed only if supported enthusiastically by the public, and they will support it only in terms of their own interests. Kennedy hit it on the head: "Hey, let's have a race to the moon!" We will be moved only by seeing Americans working and playing in space, and making money doing it. As long as the argument is whether DOD/CIA has exclusive use of space, or a few big corporations can go too, we will not be moved. When the price of a raffle ticket will buy a chance to be "The First American Nobody-Special In Space," we will get involved at the grassroots again, the money will flow, and the rockets will fly. Until then, it looks like Sergei Korolev's old John-Deere-style hardware will once again put Russia first in space.

Public Health or Animal Rights?

Being a desert community, our town has its share of problems with civil animal control. A recent proposal called for an ordinance limiting private dog ownership to four animals. More would mandate licensing as a commercial kennel. Concern about numbers of animals may draw attention to the problems of animal control, but it does not provide a solution. It seems to me the issue is whether keeping of animals constitutes a violation of rights of any individual, or of animals themselves. The correct concerns are whether the animals are a public nuisance, a health hazard, a safety hazard, or are themselves abused. Ten clean, quiet, well-cared-for, well-behaved dogs are no violation of neighbors' rights, even on a half-acre lot. One dirty, fertile, fence-jumping, garbage-slinging, cat-eating, kid-chomping howler is too many for a whole county, even if his owner has put a plum in every pocket in the County Court House, and has his license sewn into the seat of his pants. Proponents justified their actions saying, "Nobody needs more than four pets." Maybe it is true nobody needs more than four pampered baby surrogates poochie-pooping around the trailer park, but a blanket law based on such thinking does not address the needs or rights of those who live on four sections and use dogs in their ranching operations, nor of the users of canine security, nor of the responsible citizens who enjoy the profitable hobby of breeding the family dog.

The local Kennel Association defended the right of private animal-owners to compete with their own business because they savor the relationship between owner and dog, and train both in socially-responsible behavior. It is likely none who operate as professional businesses would object to a license fee as such. The problem lies not in paying the fee, but in determining who has *permission* to do so. It is a matter of how one may get—or block someone else from getting—the special use permits, environmental clearances, neighbors' release statements, noise abatement studies, etc., etc., which a responsible board of bureaucrats might eventually come to require. In pursuit of such civil power, animal control ordinances are often created as an attempt to gain broad-brush authority so that the ability of landowners to freely use their own property, to own and raise animals, and to conduct legitimate trade would be subject to the decrees of a small appointed board. Many are passed regardless of whether or not any actual violation of any person's rights was shown to have occurred. By focusing upon such limitations as numbers, breeding rights, and the like applied to all in hope of limiting the violating few, these ordinances do not address the real violations of rights at all: noise, health, safety, care, and the citizen's privacy of ownership from bureaucratic authority. It neatly avoids all of them!

Licensing does not address the problem of uncontrolled strays or wandering pets. The solution depends on first establishing a clear definition of the problem: by Animal Control, are we talking about human public health, or about animals' rights? If granting "humanitarian" rights to certain species is the objective of the publically-funded activity, then perhaps the adoptable residents of the Animal Shelter should be imposed by law upon every human family as a civic duty, like jury duty, a kind of animal affirmative action? If on the other hand, the problem is defined as control of vermin population of domestic species, nothing beats a bounty. Voluntary registration and lip-tattoo would protect owners. A dead "lipped" animal would bring a fine, not a bounty, giving bounty hunters cause for respect. A live one would bring a ransom. Folks who value their animals would protect them, and strays would be very rare.

Whether unwanted animals are eliminated by bounty hunters or by paid employees of the State, communities face expensive problems of feeding resident populations in the Animal Shelter, and disposing of thousands of euthanized animals. Except for sentimental attachment to the species, why can we not find some profitable way to recycle the tons of meat they represent, as we could if they were sheep, horses, or goats? That is abhorrent to many people, no matter how practical it may be, but it points out one significant difficulty in facing the problem. Are we solving the technical problems of animal control, or merely pandering to public emotion? We have all heard someone cluck that Hindus will starve while there are mountains of beef strolling uneaten all around them. We have hungry people in our country also, yet we still spend public money to dispose of hundreds of tons of usable food because we have a cultural taboo against eating dog and cat... even as livestock feed, or animal-shelter rations. How much of the issue of civil animal control stems from squeamish citizens' wishing certain emotion-provoking matters kept from their view? Is not "humane euthanasia" employed more to ease the shock of the observer than that of the animal?

Regardless of the means of disposal of the unwanted, the correct solution to the problem is not to restrict the rights of property owners, but instead to create laws which protect the rights of citizens from violation by their neighbors' practices or pets. These would include clear definitions of noise nuisance standards, health hazard standards, and animal care standards, and the uncontested right to trap, shoot, or otherwise dispose of any unwanted animal upon one's own property, and to use effective force in protecting one's person, family, pets, or property from attack by any animal on public property. Clearly, neither the approach of the pragmatic exterminator nor of the dewy-eyed puppy messiah can serve the needs of the entire community, but hopefully, by keeping rights of the individual citizen foremost, and tempering that reasoning with compassion for both innocent animals and sensitive people, it is possible to create a workable system which balances human social well-being, animal rights, and costs.

I like cats and dogs, but who needs a billion of them? But for that matter, who needs a billion of us? Even so, I'm still a chauvinist when it comes to my species. An attack dog with a badge on his collar is not a police officer, and don't even start about how Peaches should be able to vote, since she already eats at the table. And I won't call you Harvey Woolbanger just cause you say you're really fond of sheep.

An Open Letter To Pro-Life

I resent pro-life advocates putting words in my mouth: when I say pro-choice, that is exactly what I mean, and not pro-abortion. I believe abortion should be opposed without using criminal law, and instead with inspiration and offering positive options to the mother. It would be equally unjust of me to insist when you say pro-life, you mean pro-tyranny, for wanting to impose your choice at gunpoint by law enforcement. Reduced to simplistic form, the logic of the pro-life argument is clean and compelling: abortion is murder, and should be prohibited by enforcable law. This taken as morally fundamental, the only uncompromising resolution is total prohibition of abortion of pregnancy...for any reason whatsoever. Though protection of the unborn is the declared moral mandate of the pro-life movement, I believe very few would agree with total prohibition. More believe that certain exceptions should be made, that some pre-natal homicide is justified by their moral evaluations. These exceptions include pregnancy by rape or incest, and risk to the life of the mother. The moralist logic supporting these exclusions reveals the existence of a "hidden agenda" in the pro-life movement: not so much to protect the lives of the unborn, but to promulgate the position that sexual indulgence not intended for procreation is immoral and culpable. Abbey Lawrence of Libertarians For Life reveals the underlying moral theme: "....abortion [is] a vile act of aggression and an abdication of responsibility for the consequences of a freely chosen act...." This obligation being a matter of moral opinion, it is unjust to impose it by force of law upon others.

What about the rape exclusion? Because a woman raped did not willingly permit the sexual act which caused the pregnancy, she is not morally bound to bear the burden of parental obligation, says the rationale. The circumstances of the conception do not change the fact that any abortion is homicide. The significant factor is thus revealed to be not the life of the unborn, but the mother's moral posture at conception. Under the rape exception, the unborn must be saved if she submitted to sex for erotic pleasure, but may be aborted if she resisted sex on moral grounds. Why so, if not for her personal convenience, or the moralist posturing of her society?

What about the incest exclusion? As there is no actual harm in it, incest (that is, voluntary inter-familial copulation and breeding) is an offense only by taboo, but it is a strong and deeply felt taboo. What besides such revulsion to the moral circumstances of the conception could justify aborting the innocent unborn of such union? "What about how incest creates genetic defects?" you ask. If you would justify abortion of the unborn of an incestuous union because it *might* have genetic defects, then would you also admit abortion of an unborn shown to actually have a defect? If not, you reveal the issue is not the defects, but again the moral posture of the parents. If you would admit abortion of genetic defects, then why not terminate the defective upon identification at birth, instead of creating special care programs for them? If you would make that distinction on the basis of parturition, then you defeat your own case for pre-natal vs. post-natal rights. Further, if incest is an exclusion, would you grant legal abortion to any woman willing to testify that her father is also the child's? Would you grant freedom of choice in the death of the unborn to the willfully incestuous, where you would deny it to others? Or might you insist that the unborn may be aborted only so long as the parents are punished for sex crime? The issue is again revealed to be not foetal rights, but moral posture.

What about abortion to save the mother's life? On what grounds do you place the mother's life above that of the unborn? The unborn is innocent of its mother's suffering, and historically women died in childbirth to save the child. If unwanted pregnancy is imposed upon the woman by law as a moral obligation to accept the consequences of her voluntary copulation, then what makes her unwanted death different? If you concede death is punishment too severe for her sin of lust, so as to justify killing the innocent unborn instead, then you presume even to judge one person's suffering against another's life, and to back up your judgement with the power and might of law enforcement.

If you may create exceptions to your own rule to justify homicide by your moral evaluations, then why should not others have the right to create their own exceptions, in accordance with their moral evaluations? *What makes you so special?* **You say** the mother has a moral obligation because of her complicity in the conception. **You say** any unborn has a right to your protection by armed law enforcement from its mother's intention. **You say** your willful assumption of power over the mother's life is not only justified, it identifies you as the mother's moral superior. These contentions are all matters of opinion, no matter how serious you feel about them, or upon whose authority you choose to take them. If any exclusions are permitted, based on moral evaluation of the circumstances of conception or inconvenience to the mother, we are no longer discussing the issue of whether or not to permit legal abortion. We are only arguing over the moral grounds on which it may be justified. That is to say, if you are to base your cause upon a moral mandate to protect the lives of the unborn, then you must support total prohibition or concede you have no right at all to impose your personal judgement upon the moral decisions of others. If you would presume your moral convictions give you the right to take forcible control of the lives of others to protect their children, would you also admit the right of others to take control of your children by force of law to protect them from your choice of work, medicine, school, religion, or family structure just because they were in their own opinion morally justified? If not, your will to assume power over others for their children's sake is *self-righteous hypocrisy.*

What about total prohibition? If you would support total prohibition, subject to the full extent of law enforcement, as the War On Abortion, then the issue becomes no longer one of abstract moral or ethical questions, but of mundane practicality. To what quality of motherhood do you consign the children you would save? If you use power to take away a woman's right to control her life and body because you judge her morally unfit (as a fornicator and would-be murderer), and thus force an unwanted child upon her, should not that obligate you to fulfill the responsibility to the child that you have presumed to delegate? How can you justify leaving that child in the hands of a parent you have already judged to be morally unfit to make her own decisions? Short of raising the child yourself, the only way you could be sure you have fulfilled your duty is to insure the mother's care by official observation, regulation, and enforcement of legislated standards of parenthood. Who will set those standards? You? And how will you enforce them? Will you impose money fines upon women for being poor, ignorant, and unemployable school-dropout mothers? Will you put them in prison for trading in street crime, drugs, fencing, and whoring to feed the babies you saved? Who will care for the children then? You? Why do we not hear pro-lifers offering to take away the burdens of the unwilling mother, to bear her expenses, to feed the child, and see to its upbringing? Apart from demanding its unwelcome birth, pro-life's actions do nothing for the child, but are all directed against the mother.

If abortion is murder, how would you enforce it? If punishment is a fine, then you are only quibbling about the price of abortion, and to whom that price is paid. If you would promote imprisonment, then how long do we incarcerate a woman for seeking, attempting, or having an abortion? Would her sentence begin before or after the birth of the surviving unborn? Might a long prison sentence be grounds for granting an abortion by the staff physician? If not, do we expand our prisons into State OB wards and nurseries? If you make murder of the unborn a capital crime, who would you indict as accomplices—her doctor, parents, husband, or the manufacturer of the surgical equipment used? If abortion were crime, having a miscarriage would place a woman under suspicion of murder. If a woman miscarried as the result of an accident suffered through her voluntary exposure to risk, skiing, for example, she could be tried for manslaughter. An underground network would quickly be established among social workers and physicians to help make medically-competent secret abortion available to those who seek it in spite of the law. A second underground would also be created among the truly criminal to prey upon the same seekers. So pervasive are the requirements for monitoring and controlling such activity that only a Federal agency could have the necessary oversight and authority. Of that necessity would be born the APU, the Agency for the Protection of the Unborn.

To begin with, physicians would be obligated to report all positive pregnancy tests to the APU. Each positive test would be assigned a Social Security number, and a caseworker would monitor its progress until it was awarded a birth certificate or a legitimate obituary. Failure of any woman to obtain a test during the first trimester would constitute a misdemeanor. Since pregnancy once detected must be carried to term, employers could stand to lose valuable woman-hours as a result of their employees' moral shortcomings. Pregnancy without notice could be grounds for dismissal. Companies failing to demand periodic and random pregnancy tests of women employees could be held accountable for criminal negligence to the unborn if one of them was discovered to have had an abortion. (Just as airlines failing to demand drug tests can be held accountable if the pilot in an accident took an illegal drug). If a woman were injured or killed in an abortion attempt, her accident and life insurance would be invalid because she was committing a felony. No hospital would touch her, lest they be charged as accessary after the fact.

"Make abortion illegal and there will be no more dead babies. Women will become chaste and fathers responsible. Everything will be peachy." It is a nice dream, but an escapist fantasy. To use the law to save the lives of the unborn is a beautiful hope, but the real-life result would not be beautiful at all. Your laws would create a turbulent, crime-ridden hell in which women, their unwelcome children, and many others would be the victims. Your hope is laudable, but your desire to use power to enforce your hope is self-delusion by pride in your moral choices. We are exhorted somewhere in Scripture to accomplish God's work not by power and might, but by the Spirit. I call upon you to abandon the shortsighted expedient of force by civil law, and instead find positive ways to persuade the women you encounter to accept your reasoning and be moved in spirit to voluntarily forswear abortion and to lovingly raise their children. When you have changed their hearts, then you have done the work of God. If you are only forcing goats to behave as sheep in order to make yourself appear a better shepherd, you may be disillusioned to discover God is neither deceived nor impressed, and you shall have nothing but discord in the fold you would thus create.

Do We Have Bodily Rights?

The State presumes the citizen is his body, and as the citizen's protector, it has a duty to prevent his self-abuse of it. The Church declares he is a body with a soul to lose, and as God's anointed protector of souls, it has a sacred duty to control him to prevent his eternal damnation. Truth is, of course, every person is an eternal sovereign soul in God's universe, possessing an ephemeral body in the world. Neither is property of Church or State. Neither meretricious Church nor her incestuously-miscegenate brother State has any right to presume power in the name of protecting our bodies or souls from our own God-granted freedom of choice. That fact has not stopped them from getting into bed together, embracing the deadly sword of civil law, and establishing lifetime control over every activity any citizen might pursue. There should be no law against suicide, or assisting another, nor against self-abuse. If a joe wants to dope himself to death, let him. We have global over-population. People here have a right to stay, and to keep on breeding, but there is no purpose enforcing laws against things just because people get killed doing them. Abortion? On demand, at cost, and next-day pills at any drugstore. Yes, abortion terminates life, and masturbation is potential genocide. The self-righteous may cluck back to their chairs. No woman's body is property of Church or State such that she might be forced to commit that most personal resource against her will. Disapprove loudly as you wish, but it is between her and God, and nobody's rinkydink bizzniss. Sterilization? Likewise, on demand (or give a $50 bonus).

Is a dead body anybody's property? If people want to process bodies some particular way, they should have the right. Grandpa's mummy in the parlor, why not? Recycled body parts, unclaimed bodies, and donated ones are a resource, a wealth of transplant parts, non-specific protein byproduct, a skeleton in every biology classroom. If any service should be public, it is disposal of bodies, and health-care recycling. What's the dumbest? People die waiting for costly organs while others go in debt to pickle and bury a million bodies a year.

If our bodies are not property of the State, then the State has no right to prohibit self-abuse. Recognizing that truth demands abolishment of DEA, release of all in jail for drug crimes, and the end of all activity by any agency to detect or apprehend anyone for use or production of unpatented or natural drugs. Likewise, acknowledging our right and responsibility for our bodies' wellbeing lies with ourselves and not the government calls for abolishment of the Bureau of Alcohol, Tobacco, and Firearms. Alcohol can be made by anyone with the recipe, and should not be regulated. If it is OK for one joe to sell beer, any joe should be free to sell beer, out of his basement like Amway soap. For all its known harmfulness, tobacco should not be the subject of government regulation—along with marijuana, opium, coca, peyote, psilocybin, comfrey, or vitamin Z. If our souls are not Church property, and the Constitution forbids imposing its doctrine through law, then right demands revocation of all "blue laws". If it is OK to sell beer on Saturday, it is OK to sell it Sunday. If it is OK down the street, it is OK next to the church, or the gun store. Firearms? The Constitution forbids restricting our right to arm ourselves. All laws limiting our right to own weapons should be revoked. The right to use force defending your body or other property should be absolute. However, punishment for initiating force against an innocent should be severe. Kill somebody in a robbery, lets weed the gene pool of you, now. Use deadly force to compel submission, you're in the cage with the boogeyman, bozo, and we put the videos on late-night TV. Capital trials should be a public event. In the rainforest, cannibalism by the community is used as capital punishment. Man, that is pure! You've got some joe up for capital crime. Come jury time, you strap him into the chair center stage. Each juror votes by pushing a Yes or No button. If there are enough Yes votes to convict, the perp is fried on the spot. If not, he walks out a free man. Would that be sane and just? Not likely, which might actually make a better deterrent. Nobody wants to star on "Judgement Day," and people are lining up to be jurors.

Suicide, Slavery, and Sin

Saw a bumper sticker: "Kevorkian for President". We might better make him the President's health aide... Government policy toward suicide again reveals the presumption that our bodies are property of the state, to be protected (or as with the draft, expended) even if in opposition to our personal will, as it suits the Suits in DC. How is it not clear to everyone that every human being has the right to terminate his life? It is after all, his body, her body, your body... not their body. It has been made Constitutional law that no person in America may own another person. Opposition to slavery is one thing people of all races here agree with. But if the government is just a group of individuals who have gained a position to wield collective power, why should they have the right to own persons? How is it that in so many ways, they presume to own our bodies, and to treat us all as incarcerated slaves? They proclaim it is for our own good, and therefore for the good of the collective that they should use the power of the gun—law enforcement—to take from us the right to behave as free citizens with respect to our own bodies. Is the slavemonger who forces his slaves to exercise his notions of good health and fitness (so they will be good collective workers) any less a slavemonger, or does his generosity to his slaves justify his ownership? Even if government kept us all fat and safe from risk, would that justify its taking away our right to choose to be something else, even if to our own destruction? Unfortunately, many seem happy being fat and stimulated, put to work and taxed to create the Massa' State that feeds and medicates them and makes all their hard choices for them. The policies of the present government are totally committed to the proposition that your body, soul, and property are the responsibility of the government to be observed, documented, regulated, and manipulated, at the point of a gun when it is expedient for the controllers. Both Republican and Democrat politicians will continue this policy if people continue to vote them into office.

The roots of authoritarian opposition to suicide are politically influenced by the large money flows associated with insurance and probate, and as always, supported by those who believe suicide to be sin, and who feel they must therefore do whatever necessary to others in order to protect their souls. Taking their sect's edition of God's Laws in one hand, and the might of civil enforcement in the other, they proclaim themselves by virtue of their moral superiority their brothers' keepers. Here's the straight word on that subject: God's laws cannot be broken. Not "may not" but *cannot.* That which we can do, does not violate God's law. All those rules about whether or not we *may* do that which we have "free will" to do are just that—rules somebody decided to proclaim and enforce. Good ideas, lots of them, but not God's laws. If you can be persuaded to believe you are guilty of violating God's law by your act, you can be controlled, and led to make payments of propitiation in both substance and deed. Gravity is a good example of God's law. We did not get to the moon by violating that divine law, but by obeying it perfectly. Orbital physics is a manifestation of God's law, "What goes around comes around." This law is clearly observable in the Vedic notion of karma, and in the cyclicity of the I Ching, even if obscured by the Biblical paradigm of commandment, disobedience, and punishment vs. divine gratuitousness toward the awled-eared obedient slave. If as the moralist authoritarians say, God is down on suicide, then it is surely between that soul and God, and not the business of self-appointed Divine Judges in the world.

Personally, I think anybody who needs to call a doctor to help him kill himself is short a couple of organs to begin with, not to mention imagination and a sense of adventure. But even giving them that, why should there be a question of whether a doctor may do it? Why not anyone? The government's right to grant the doctor's sacred exclusive privilege to practice medicine is based upon the presumption that the government is protecting the collective patient from quacks. In the case of assisted suicide, a practitioner could only be rightly called a quack if the patient survived. If we have the right to own our own bodies, and to dispose of them, we should have the right not only to the assistance of a doctor, but of anyone we might wish to choose to be with us in such a profound moment.

"We'll Protect You, Body and Soul."

When a gambler and his kid go to the casino, the kid is forbidden to operate the gambling machines, and graciously provided with non-gambling entertainment. The gambler sits in front of a video, feeds quarters into a slot, and is entertained with games of skill and luck. The kid sits in front of a video, feeds quarters into a slot, and is likewise entertained. According to the "moralist" viewpoint, the gambler's play is vice, an immoral thing to which only a responsible adult should have even limited access, and the other an appropriate activity for the chiiildren whom they would presume to protect from temptation. The only difference between the games is that the gambler's machine gives him a chance to use skill and luck to win, whereas the kid's machine takes every quarter every time.

Whether or not things like sex, drugs, and gambling are immoral should certainly be a matter of personal opinion. They should not be the subject of any enforced government opinion. If individuals or the members of any sect, party, or other group believe a particular activity is immoral, they are guaranteed the right by the Constitution to say so openly. If they choose to eschew those activities in their lives, they are free to do that without infringing upon anyone's right to their moral opinions, and without involving the power and might of law enforcement. But beyond that, the presumption that everyone must be forced to eschew them likewise is most unrighteous.

Purveyors of forgiveness must persuade their market to believe they are guilty. The priesthood may not be the oldest profession, but it is certainly the oldest racket. If you believe you are damned by somebody else's "original" sin, you can be sold anything to get you off the hook. Anything we might enjoy—but lowing praise to an authoritarian idol— is at least suspected of having roots in sin, and therefore any desire for pleasure should motivate the penitent to conviction. If one can be made to believe his most precious God-given natural pleasures are evil, and his desire evidence condemning him to eternal whatever-you-fear-the-most, he can be made to subject himself, and sacrifice his estate. It is spiritual blackmail.

Here is a clear index by which the use of State power can be seen to be unrighteous: *your body and your soul are not the property of the State.* The State has no righteous authority to protect your body as though it were government property, by taking over your life by force. All of the laws against "self-abuse"—the penal occupation of America through the Drug War—presume the right to forcibly take control of your body to protect it from you. Likewise the laws against prostitution, pornography, and personal non-standard sex deny the right of the individual citizen to willingly grant to another citizen any level of access to his or her body, for whatever reason or reward is mutually agreeable. Whose body is it? Do you believe your body is Federal Property?

Why does the State presume to meddle forcibly in these areas of our lives? Because of an even more insidious presumption. They have a "moral obligation" to the community, and therefore not only a right, but a mandate. To begin with, there is no such thing as a community— there are only us individuals. To say the community may be protected from abuse by taking the rights from its individuals is hardly different from saying the forest may be protected from fire by cutting down all the trees. Though protecting your body from abuse with drugs is a practical objective, morality is not so derived. Most precisely, morality has to do with one's perceived state of grace before God. When a well-intentioned but self-righteous (or sect-righteous) zealot presumes himself to be the spiritual guardian of his fellow man, he is seeking to prevent spiritual self-abuse, seeking to protect your soul, as though it were his to protect. "The Soul is God's," I hear someone bleat. Yes, which fact does not make it the property of any religious institution, no matter how deeply they believe their bigotry to be equivalent to faith. Therefore when a religious body takes upon itself to bed down with the kings of the earth, to seize the deadly sword of civil law, and to impose its doctrine and taboo upon all by force, its acting in the name of protecting our souls is presumptuously blasphemous.

If our government in its self-proclaimed desire to improve our lives were as honest and generous to the citizen as the casino industry is to its customers, and respected our personal rights to our lives, our private pleasures, and our property like the casinos do, our candidates for office would not need to sell their loyalty to buy ad time on TV to get out the vote.

Memorial In Vain

I write this on Memorial Day. Yes, I know, yesterday's holiday is old news, and therefore no news. We take our Federally-mandated free day's pay, put away the Flag, and go back to the "Veterans' issues…ho-hum" attitude we maintain the other 364. I'm a veteran, with the Distinguished Flying Cross, among other honorable decorations. Though I hold my service in high regard, and belong to several veterans' organizations, I am not able to comfortably attend meetings of most. I am too often gently rebuked for being "political" instead of maintaining the posture toward God and Flag expected of the soldier. To my thinking, a soldier who does not know or agree to the politics of those who command him is an amoral mercenary, no matter how pious and honorable he may be, or how glorious the government which hires or conscripts him. A soldier who willingly fights unto death, confident he knows his leaders' righteous principles, is spiritually fulfilled and a champion in the world, you can take that from me. It is a fine feeling to fight for a righteous cause, even if in retrospect the cause you trusted seems less noble than at the time.

The professional soldier and the veteran I believe should be more "political" than others, since they are the ones who must go (or send their sons) to kill other people because of their politics. If a soldier is pious, and truly concerned for his soul, it would seem important his homicide be done for righteous reasons. If having pledged to obey The

Flag, he sees his leaders' actions are immoral, or hypocrisy, he must make a critical decision—whether patriotism means defending the rights and principles which define the country, or defending the regime holding the authoritarian offices, regardless of their violation of those principles. If the leaders' attitude is, "Victory is worth suspending the rights and principles for which we fight," then any moralist justification is merely expedient propaganda. Defensive war is morally moot—if they come, you fight. They sink your navy, you sink their island, budda-boom. However, attacking a country in the name of defending a principle is not defensive war, right or wrong. It is police action, authoritarian political aggression. When we justify sending fighters to kill people to defend their rights from their bad political regimes, then deny them and our own citizens those same rights that define us as a nation, we make murderous hypocrites of ourselves. By any standard I know of, that is immoral. If our Bill Of Rights is what justifies us, we damn sure better be getting those rights at home, and seeing to it all the people we "save" get those rights too.

I am no longer able to recite the Pledge of Allegiance. We are taught as children to drone, "I plejaleejus tuda flag…" without knowing what it means. The Flag is a symbol of authority, and to pledge allegiance means to promise to subject oneself and obey. That's a fine idea, but our judges at Nuremberg all agreed the individual German was not absolved of personal moral failing by having faithfully given allegiance to his Flag. "…and to the Republic for which it stands," is still all right with me, if I take that to mean as the Constitution defines it, and not the corrupt and oppressive structure of greed, pride, and power festering in Washington DC. I do NOT pledge allegiance to the Flag. I pledge allegiance to the Constitutional principles which a certain group of British subjects made traitors, outlaws, and terrorists of themselves to grant to their heirs and to history. I'm with them. They got it right, POLITICALLY. When our government—"The Flag" we are to owe allegiance—rapes us of those rights for which the Veterans died, and imposes upon us the socialist police policies of the regimes they died to defeat, then all those honored dead have died in vain.

Lots of flame going around about the New World Order, a conspiracy to impose some global regime. As an American patriot, I am pretty wary of seeing the USA swallowed up as one more Free Peoples' State in the United Sodality of Terra. My trepidation comes from observing that seems to be occurring, perhaps inevitably, but it is not a Bill Of Rights world they are forming. The present US government is clearly directed toward such globalism, and also clearly directed toward a highly-policed socialism as its format. If I saw my government standing up in the world demanding that every country unite to grant every citizen every right in the Bill Of Rights, repealing every law in every country starting with THIS country which abridge or violate those rights... well, fellows, this old rotorhead burnout would RE-UP!

Our Flags: Burn the Ban.

The movement to amend the Constitution to ban burning the Stars and Stripes as a political statement is well-intentioned, but a terrible mistake. Our flag is a symbol of a special relationship between citizen and state: the voluntary loyalty of free private individuals. I was taught in Army officer training that obedience can be compelled, but respect must be earned. If a citizen may be prosecuted for disrespect toward a symbol of freedom, then his right to any dissent is eroded, and the flag is thus truly tarnished. How sad when the right to make public statements against the government is being newly granted in Russia to see that right attacked in America. When a politician wraps himself in the flag, then calls for a law against flag-burning, what is he really trying to protect? Would a flag-burning amendment also prohibit shredding the flag as a statement against covert government? How about throwing acid on the flag to protest toxic pollution, or staining the flag pink as a statement against pro-socialist sentiment in Congress? How about such disrespectful acts as burning the President in effigy, or peeing on The Wall we Vietnam veterans hold sacred? Surely these are deplorable acts, but where the rights protecting such declarations of political opinion are absent in the world, it is there we declare oppressive government exists, and where we feel most justified in sending our soldiers as "defenders of freedom." If in the name of defending the flag we abandon those rights, we shall have lost the battle for freedom without even facing an enemy.

The enslaved may be compelled to obey—the free must be inspired. So let the dogs bark at the flag, and if they tear it down, raise high another. Let us stand firm as champions of personal liberty throughout the world to defend others' right to yell insults and cast dung at any icon of power, and when those who see this are moved to revulsion for those who desecrate symbols, and respect for those who defend rights, then our purpose will have truly prevailed.

As a combat veteran, I proudly fly the Stars and Stripes, but I certainly did not, nor would I ever fight for "The Flag". I fought, and would fight again against any enemy, to preserve those principles of responsible freedom for which I was taught the flag stands. As a libertarian refinement of a democratic Constitution, the Bill Of Rights is a pinnacle of achievement in applied social philosophy. It is unique in that it is intended not to impose limitations on the citizen, but instead to guarantee that statist limitations shall not be imposed. Those who promote the No-Burn Amendment wish to add to the Constitution not another guarantee of liberty, but a punitive restriction of political expression. They would make of the flag a symbol not of civil freedom, but of enforced display of civil obedience. The movement is an attempt to rally the unthinking around the flag as a symbol of patriotic obedience, where they lack commitment to an issue that might mobilize an informed citizenry—a practice sometimes called jingoism. As such, the Jingo Amendment is the antithesis of those principles for which the flag stands.

Equally offensive is the recent movement to ban the display of the flag of the Confederacy, as a "symbol of racism". The Civil War was not fought over slavery—which was an issue, but hardly THE issue. As any knowledgeable southerner will point out, that terrible holocaust was fought by the Confederacy in defense of the Constitutionally-defined rights of the sovereign states to regulate their own internal affairs without forced intervention by the Federal government. Those who fly the Stars and Bars do so in respect for those long-abridged states' rights. No American today would stand up for the practice of racist slavery—so should we therefore ban Federal Reserve Notes because they bear portraits of American Presidents whose administrations permitted slavery?

The First Amendment guarantees the right of an American to display or desecrate ANY symbol as a statement of his or her personal opinion. If that freedom is sacrificed to prevent destruction of any such symbol as a statement of political dissent, *then* is the American flag truly desecrated. If the libertarian spirit of the Bill of Rights is not kept alive in the United States of America, then that great document becomes only the hemp linen shroud in which the greatest political experiment in the history of mankind is mummified for the historians—and perhaps the hopeful idealists—of another day. This is our day. Let us not lose it. Defend what each of those gallant banners have once stood for: our Constitutional guarantees of personal freedom, states' rights, and voluntary loyalty to a righteous representative government.

Affirmative Action in the White House?

Equality of opportunity is neither a fact nor the law in America. There is individual prejudice among people of all racial groups against others, and the result of such prejudice is cruel and unjust in every case. Though well-intentioned, perhaps even pragmatically correct at one point in our history, the laws collectively known as "affirmative action" give discriminatory precedence to some people by race, in the name of eliminating the practice of giving precedence to some people by race. Though the severe inequity suffered by blacks and others in our past (and in spite of enormous progress, still suffered today) deserves righting, AA was not in practice a move toward racial justice, but instead is a sacrifice of the rights of certain white people, done to mollify minorities' desire for revenge against their ancestors. In the name of justice (but for the purpose of organizing minority groups into manipulable voting masses), the rich whites in power gave away neither their rights nor privileges, but the rights and jobs of lower class whites. The AA laws stripped working-class whites of a precious American heritage, that same heritage which was cruelly denied to non-whites once, but which white social activists the last forty years have gone to such trouble to guarantee to others: the right to compete fairly for the advantages of success in America with equal opportunity, without discrimination against them for race or color.

Open competition may not always produce racially-equal results. Does anyone suppose Evander Holyfield and Venus Williams are where they are today because of some affirmative action law obligating white athletes to take a dive if up against a minority competitor? Or should white athletes demand such a law to give them "a fighting chance at equality" against the (naturally superior?) black champions? Since the concept has been expanded to include other forms of "disadvantage" besides just race—such as gender, age, handicap, etc—there is only one group of Americans who do not have some kind of demographic category around which they can rally politically to seek laws specifically "protecting the equal rights" of themselves as opposed to those of other demographics. In each case of "protection" it is assumed that the "minority" needs its rights defended, while the "non-minority" is presumed to need no defense. More and more, the view is taken that our rights inhere not in our being individual citizens, but in the demographic group to which we belong. Every protection program excludes the same group, the SWABWAM …the straight, white, able-bodied, working-age male… who is presumed to be an arrogant, exploitive elitist, a sexist, racist villain… and rich.

In city, state, or any other government-regulated job, these laws mean when a swabwam applies, any applicant of the correct minority is given "cuts" ahead of him. Where taxpayer-funded "internships" will pay half a job's wage if the employer will hire an otherwise-unqualified applicant from some particular minority group, employers will go looking for one, and agree to teach her the job before they will pay the full wage to hire a non-minority regardless of his qualifications, or how hard he studied and worked to acquire them. (Consider how highschool students might feel about this fact.) To fulfill mandatory "quotas," the AA lawmakers have criminalized fair employee-qualifying process in labor law. Even if an employer is truly non-discriminatory, the law takes away his right to select his employees in his own business to suit his own choices, and imposes its racially-specific decisions upon him.

If affirmative action is as the Congress and the Justices have said, the fair, just, and lawful thing to do down at the working-class level, then let's see how they like it. In the name of racial justice and equality, let us dispense with the Presidential Election. Why should it be different in the White House? Let us not forget that so far 100% of the holders of that job have been white, and a quota of even 1% would at this point obligate the Electoral College to select the "best qualified ethnic-minority candidate." We could just save the American people all those tax-paid campaign millions, and free the TV sets of politics the whole year in favor of the ball games we find so much more important anyway, by invoking the laws of affirmative action, and just giving the job to the first candidate of the most-politically-correct minority group who shows up. Forget Al Gore, Son Of Bush, and Harry Browne—in the name of affirmative action for racial equality at all class levels, lets just give the job to Jesse Jackson… or Dennis Rodman, or Whoopi Goldberg. Heck, I'd VOTE for Whoopi!

Really Cut Government Spending?

Art: Eliminate the NEA, and all government activity which judges or regulates the artistic, moral, political, or other merits of literature or art, other than needed for the architecture of government facilities.

Social Security: Offer voluntary freedom from FICA tax by waiving rights to benefits. Base receipt of non-taxed benefits on need, to provide subsistence to the elderly, not guaranteed gravy for the able.

Defense Industry: Give necessary defense industry something else to do. Improve by redirecting money for parallel civilian purposes. Examples: pursue space for commercial success. Get security and liability concerns out of the way of anyone who can make money in space—feature films, tourism, industrial colonies in orbit or on the moon; develop military-usable water, waste treatment, and alternative-energy systems for homes, companies, and small communities; maintain a large Corps of Engineers manpower pool for disaster and environmental projects, including civil construction, toxic waste dumps, highway cleanup, etc; create an Army "Alien Corps", in which refugees can work under discipline, learn English, American culture and basic laws, to be granted citizenship upon completion of a tour of duty; expand military hospitals and medical schools, make them available to all veterans, dependents, identified disaster victims, etc, and price their services at cost, in direct competition with the physician/insurance monster.

Contracts: Mandate in the budget of any contractor accepting Federal funds that no individual's salary may exceed that of the President of the United States. No CEO, hot-shot engineer, genius ad-flack, nor celebrity endorsing the product on TV should be more highly paid on any government-contract job.

Drugs: Eliminate all funds to subsidize tobacco. Eliminate funding for drugs prescribed not to cure illness, but only to give the patient an artificial sense of wellness, including tranquilizers, anti-depressants, and sedatives. Decriminalize marijuana. Don't tax it, regulate it, prescribe it, or otherwise mandate control of its natural market. Drop all marijuana cases, grant presidential pardon to all marijuana offenders, and release them. Terminate funding for surveillance, apprehension, and prosecution of marijuana traffic. Economic advantages: empty half our prisons; end billions flowing out of our country to buy a crop we can profitably grow; end billions more given to governments of pot-growing nations to oppress their people with para-military narc forces; open the market to the benefits of hemp, including non-acid paper, livestock feed, and environmentally-beneficial replacements for petro-chemical fibers. Grant prescribed access to heroin. We permit such medical addiction now to tranquilizers, sleeping pills, and sedatives sold on a perpetual basis to millions. This will bring the opium market under competitive pressure, breaking the power structure of organized crime now supplying the demand. The greatest benefit would be eliminating small-time criminals who now prey upon the common citizen to supply themselves. This benefit is a decrease in the expense of law enforcement and insurance claims. If any drug should be outlawed, it is cocaine. Unfortunately, making it a black-market commodity multiplies its power to do evil many times. As a democracy of concerned individuals and responsible government, we must find a way to treat cocaine as a personal behavior problem, and not as a criminal disobedience problem.

Churches: In accordance with the Constitutional requirement that government shall not respect institutions of religion, terminate their tax-exempt status. Churches should pay full taxes on all revenues made through the sale of religious tracts, sacrificial items, or religious practitioner services. Why should this not extend to our foreign policy? Provide no "foreign aid" to any institution of world religion, even if it may have gained the trappings of statehood, including the Vatican, Israel, all Islamic governments, or any such nation in which civil power is vested in a religious sect.

Public School: Education should be available to all eligible children at government expense. It should be neither mandatory nor "guaranteed", but a voluntary privilege. Curricula should be strictly secular and empirical. Children who fail to conform to standards of behavior or performance could be denied attendance. It should be very easy to license private schools, and to operate them as businesses in competition with other educators. The choice of private curricula should be agreed upon between the schools and parents, and not made to conform to any standards established by government. No public money should be paid for the attendance of any student in a private school, whether parochial or secular.

Though Americans call for reduced government spending, very few mean it. The most common position is probably, "Cut off that freeloader over there—and fund my deserving program."

Prison, Punishment, and Public Good

Why put people into prison? To punish them, to make them better citizens, to deter others, and to protect others from them. Punishment for its own sake is pointless moral exercise. It makes sense only as corrective improvement of the individual, or as a deterrent, a step toward improvement in the public. The usual punishments are fines, denial of rights, imprisonment, and death. Fines are good punishment, particularly for crimes of acquisition. The problem is temptation for individuals or agencies in power to make arrests to seize assets for themselves. Fines and punitive property seizure cause the crime of robbery by prosecution, corruption which can exist only within the system of law enforcement, causing net destruction to the public good. Denial of rights, such as disenfranchisement, inability to get bonding, insurance, security clearance, etc, makes it more difficult for the punished to rejoin the public. Denied access to legitimate enterprise, they are more likely to seek anti-social activities, making them more dangerous than before punishment. The policy is net destructive to the public good. The forced isolation of incarceration is also good punishment, but with destructive potential. The difference lies in creation of unpleasant conditions in prison as punishment—that is, torture. Forcing prisoners together in fear and hate under the oppression of violent guards is definitely punishment, but the effect on the subjects is destructive. The effect of teaching "jailhouse mentality" to large numbers of citizens (particularly the young) is net destructive to the public good. The problem with punishment as a deterrent to future crime is the inherent injustice of "making an example" by punishing the individual for the imagined future crimes of others. The presumed deterrent is the would-be offender's fear, and though the public may accept it, it is nonetheless injustice to the individual. Punishment done to inspire fear of the law is statist terrorism, exactly the practice identified as villainy in Darth Vader (chief of Imperial security, enforcing law without tolerance). Where that is acknowledged, soon grows the seed of resentment and distrust of government—which breakdown of confidence is net destructive to the public good.

As protection of the public from the subject, execution is absolute. As punishment, death is either best or worst. If the most severe punishment is a lifetime of torture, death might be a merciful option. Merciful also, yet punishing indeed might be isolation without media, mail, phone, visitors, or any other contact. However, if the objective of temporary incarceration is truly "corrective" as advertised, then the effect upon the subject should clearly be improvement in attitude toward himself, the public, and the law. If the effect is instead clearly destructive to the subjects' social potential, then for what reason perpetuate the practices? If the objective is to accrue something to the public good by the tax expenditure, surrender of public rights, and damage to the lives of the imprisoned, then those practices which have a net destructive effect might best be stopped, and practices which best accomplish advantage to the public good be kept or initiated. Short of executing dangerous offenders, protecting the public is best done by imprisonment, the longer sentence the better. The public is protected as long as the subject is isolated, whether tortured or living in luxury. Since the socially-destructive effects of jail result from harsh conditions created as punishment, perhaps the most beneficial practice might be to reverse that. Prison life costs taxpayers $40,000 per year. How many of us have that to live on? Jail could be cheaper using less security, and more luxury. When the point is reached where jail is better than life outside, there is a curious incentive to stay. If indefinite sentence in a soft cell is cheaper than a carousel of crime, arrest, prosecution, and high-security lockup, if the public is protected, and the prisoner has a better life than ever, where is the objection? Why not turn old apartment neighborhoods into high-surveillance cell blocks where prisoners have TV, recreation, and a Vegas buffet, if it meant greater public security at lower public cost? Add work, beer, choice of Valium or marijuana, and overnight visitation, and some folks might forget they were in prison. Some might even call it a workable social format. Everybody has a debt to the State, as public servant or public offender. Everybody has a cell, job assignment, check-in schedule, and mess-hall pass. All that's need is for everybody either to be guilty of some crime, or to have taken State employment maintaining the comfortable residence blocks, and controlling the lives of those who live there. Add slot machines and a sports book and, hey, maybe The Millennium has arrived after all.

Freedom Schmeedom.
It's Over.

I'll say it again: the golden age of liberty in America is over, and nobody misses it. The Constitution is only middle-school mumbo-jumbo to most Americans, a few questions to be answered on a Social Studies test and then forgotten. Few could state the freedoms from government granted by the Bill of Rights, beyond "freedom of speech, separation of church and state, and the right to bear arms," all of which are flagrantly violated by the Cult of Power in Washington in numerous ways, all supported by the courts and enforced with lethal power. Worse, all of the violations are accepted as justified exceptions by the overwhelming majority of Americans. The minorities crying most loudly for freedom still vote for state-created jobs and increased entitlements and benefits from Massa Washington. The gun-rights nuts swear they will kill or die for the Second Amendment, but they vote for martially-armed law enforcement for prohibition of personal rights proclaimed immoral by the politically-predominant church. The abusive use of guns by citizens and by uniformed agents of the State is escalating, and the desire of government and large masses of socialized citizens is to take the guns away from those the masses fear, and leave only the occupying military power of law enforcement armed to protect us all. The result can only be a three-way fight between the heavily-armed genuine criminal out to prey on the citizen, the citizen who arms himself unlawfully in self-defense, and the armies of Darth Metro's Ubiquitous Security, for each of whom the other two are deadly enemies. Another group which whines impotently about the genuine abuses of our rights and freedoms is the Drug War protesters. Since the generation that first protested drug persecution also protested against the Vietnam War, the WWII generation concluded drug protesting is unpatriotic. Since those young freedomists also led in the sex revolution, their elders in power concluded drug use leads to immorality. Having lived in the drug underground for some time in my life, I know personally all the common shit and the lifestyles of the users of each. I wouldn't claim any of it is any good, but the government's draconian War has caused a hundred times more damage to our country than the combined effects of all of it. I recommend we all get off the stuff, from America's number-one killer, tobacco, the insidious ego-inflater cocaine, mind-numbing heroin, even the relatively harmless mild euphoric marijuana, and particularly all of the tranquilizers, sedatives, mood-enhancers, anti-depressants, uppers and downers, and such synthetic garbage your benevolent legal pill-pusher Dr. Feelgood will happily prescribe for you. Making it all legal might end the damage of the Drug War, but only we ourselves can end the damage drugs cause, legal or not, so clean up your act.

The Holy War On Drugs has been the single most destructive influence on the knowledge and practice of Constitutional freedom in America's history. As with Hitler's Jews, the enemy in that cruel war is the private citizen, and the purpose of his persecution is the creation of the security state. If the urine sample we are forced to surrender on demand to employer, Dean of Students, or police were tested for DNA instead of devil weed, our racial groups could be immediately identified, so that nobody could lie about his race to get on welfare... or any other reason the government might like to impose. The last Presidential Election was settled by a few hundred votes. Since even the simple possession of the most common and least harmful of the forbidden substances is by law a felonious disobedience, the Drug War has disenfranchised millions of Americans as felons. Marijuana is used as a litmus test for those who might make up their own minds about how reasonable any particular law might be, and who might decide not to do something just because some board of puffed-up professional power-freaks with law degrees write a rule saying they must. A dope felon never votes again, even if too young to vote when convicted. The potential dissident, the free thinker, is identified, and systematically disenfranchised, leaving to vote only those who have proved they will take the law as fundamentalists, and obey it. Would two million re-enfranchised free-thinking marijuana felons have made a significant difference in the last election? No, whether they all voted for Harry Browne or not. No, because both of The Major Parties will conduct the business of Government the same way. Both the Left and the Right will perpetuate the Drug War, Social Security, the IRS, ATF, ETC, and the general growth of the authoritarian wealth-distribution and behavior-control mechanism of the welfare police state in America. The system is two-fisted, one hand cupped supporting the citizen, the other cupped over it confining him. The difference between the Republicans and the Democrats? Turn the hands over. You're in good hands now, Schmuckos.

I Resign

I once thought myself some kind of prophet crying out warning in the wilderness, but it seems I have only been pissing into the wind. Congress has made laws respecting establishments of religion, from oppressive blue laws, prayer healing on Medicare, drug use made legal for a particular race's church, even granting certain religions recognized political states supported by our taxes. Some are opposed by calling them cults, or supported by calling them faith-based organizations, and some respected by making their mythology equivalent to science in school, while prohibiting them to celebrate on public grounds. Freedom of speech is abridged by making certain words illegal if addressed to uniformed agents of State, calling other words hate-crime if applied to persons darker than the speaker, or calling words legally spoken conspiracy if someone is present to hear them. People may assemble peaceably, unless to petition for redress of grievances, or are young members of ethnic groups declared to be gangs of criminals. Leaders of well-regulated militia are persecuted, and strident efforts to disarm the people fill newspapers every day. Dogs are being trained to locate guns, and even where right to possess a gun is still respected, it is illegal to fire it. The right to be secure against unreasonable search has long passed, as any search is considered reasonable if the word "drugs" is uttered by an agent of State or his dog, while government gluts itself upon seizure of property any suspect of drug crime may own, failure to convict notwithstanding. Just compensation for property taken is just whatever government decides to pay. Public trial is what the jury gets to see after the lawyers have decided what part of the evidence presented to them is admissible, and perversion of the process of jury selection prevents the impartial from being seated. Powers not delegated to government are presumed its privilege upon recognition, and there is no area of human activity which any agent of government will declare definitively to belong to the people, and to no agency of State. Such abstract concepts as reason, righteousness, and reality have no bearing, if they conflict with process, precedent, admissibility, celebrity, or money. Such concepts are likewise dismissed in the system of discipline used in schools, so upcoming generations are accustomed to the summary judgement of deans and boards, and do not expect more as adults from the wardens and nannies of the State. It is in our schools that destruction of all Constitutional protection of the people from the State is seen most clearly. The presumption that children must be protected by government authority has been taken in such fundamental sense that the *a priori* presumption they are property of State is not even examined. Parents too are now subject to punitive commands of school bureaucrats, without recourse. Disciplinary process is entirely prosecutorial, and there exists in the school system no person whose office is to defend the rights of student or parent against its machinations, no matter how those may conflict the letter or intention of Constitutional rights. It is hardly fair, however, to blame the schools, churches, or officers of government for these grievances. It is clear almost all Americans are content with the way things have developed, and are prepared to vote and behave in support of the welfare police State. We have long cried warning of the walls closing in as the authoritarian left reduced individual rights in the name of collective well-being, and the authoritarian right reduced rights in the name of collective morality. As indicated by the recent election, the walls have met in the middle, and less than two percent voted for the only party calling for defense of Constitutional freedom. We all drink our favorite of two brands of cola, wear our favorite of two brands of rubber shoes, and vote for our favorite of the two brands of Massa Washington's socialism. The Chief Justice of the Supreme Court recently stated the most important issue facing him is the need to increase the salary of federal judges. We have all become good Nazis in office or good niggers in jail, proud public servants, fat dumb cattle, or criminals locked down and shut up for correctional therapy. The greatest experiment in political freedom in the history of mankind is over. Welcome to your Animal Farm, friends, I'm retiring the pen.

The Ego Rallies,
But For What?

Publisher Mark says I am a tired old crybaby feeling sorry for myself because I figure I am wasting my breath casting parlance before the fattened masses of brain-dead US Federal livestock who don't give a pickled poot about the passing of our Constitutional freedoms. Knowing he is right chafes the ego enough I am compelled to take another shot at it, so I press this upon his indulgence and attempt a comeback. Questions that come to mind are, "Whom should I try to rally, against whom or what should we rally, what should we do to reclaim our freedoms, and what should we do when we've got them back?" Perhaps a more important question is, "Do we really need them?" If our Founders established the Bill of Rights so Americans might live long and prosper, it is hard to object to today's America. In the history of mankind, nobody has ever had more of anything than we have. Perhaps my concern is more for the future, observing that when you stand at the top of the pyramid, every step you take can lead to a fall.

To whom do I cry my Cassandra's warning? We are all divided into demographic voting blocs, each told some "right" (socialist entitlement) can be obtained for our own group by agreeing to some thus-justifiable limitation of the "privileges" (Constitutional rights) of all. The results have been predictable, though largely unspeakable. The racial group most loudly (and justly) crying for freedom the last forty years are blacks. Led by various demagogues and agitators to demand greater and greater benefits at the Federal trough, they have produced two generations of welfare-addicted, illegitimate, illiterate, irresponsible, crime-ridden, and violent people turning once-affluent communities from which they were previously barred into barren slums wherein they prey most cruelly upon each other, a terrible waste of a very fine bloodline of human beings. To use Paul McCartney's line, Brothers, you got your lucky break, and you broke it. For all the good those who like myself hate racism in any form might wish for you, nobody can fix it but yourselves. Don't waste your time whining to Massa Washington, who will only feed you crumbs with one hand for being good niggers, and whup you with the other when you get bad. Likewise for Hispanics, Indians, women, old folks, and the like whose leaders are trying to get you organized to vote for them by tempting you with chile, low-fat sugar, or Viagra on your cornbread for getting in line with the blacks. Only one group of Americans may not join together to whine about some alleged disadvantage, so as to obtain legislation to win a place closer to the Federal trough. Those are straight, white, able-bodied, working-aged males (like myself), whose attempt to do that would earn instant censure as homophobic, racist, uncaring, exploitive, sexist villains—precisely the image necessary for any of the other whiners to obtain their objectives. So we have nothing to gain by bitching either.

If the "enemies" of freedom are as they seem, the self-serving pork-fed career politicians chumming the masses with subsistence welfare to protect the privileged corporate barons who own them, self-righteous dominionist preachers promulgating the idolatry of their authoritarian cults of guilt and sacrifice, correctional-institution-minded school administrators brainwashing the young with statist propaganda and behavioral conditioning, less-than-zero-tolerant hanging judges and the eager and arrogant guard dogs of their law enforcement armies, racist agitators elevating themselves on the shoulders of masses gathered around banners of their own skin color in hatred of all others, and hordes of amoral lawyers, lobbyists, and legislators willing to defend or attack any person or position regardless of righteousness or reality for the right fee… if these are the enemies of freedom, then what might be done by the letter of any law to defeat them? Since they own the law, the schools, the money, and the power, looks to me like: nothing. What might be done by working "within the system" of electoral process, which clearly has been usurped by the media-perfected techniques of marketing celebrity? As evidenced by the pathetic dribble of votes for the Bill-Of-Rights-based Libertarian Party: nothing. What might be accomplished by the selective or general assassination of any or all of the above? As evidenced by the tragic folly of bombing—or even resisting—Federal forces: nothing. If we have all become like ants milking the honey from our aphids on the high green branches of a burning bush, then what can we do to save ourselves, our children, or the political principles which brought us to our present state of affluence? Nothing? So you tell me, friends, am I just pissing into the wind, and likely to have it thrown back into my face by all of those above mentioned, or can you say I am doing anyone any good? And while you're thinking about that, what are you doing about it?

About the Author

James was born Aquarius 1943, raised near White Sands, New Mexico, Republican son of a rocket radio engineer and an artist. In high school a science-fair winner, thespian, and president of Chess and Writing clubs, he became a winning swimmer, gymnast, and martial artist in college. After two years at remote New Mexico Tech studying geophysics, he dropped out in 1963 to enter Marine Corps jet pilot training. He eventually served as a helicopter gunship pilot with the 101st Airborne in Viet Nam, where he was highly decorated, including the Distinguished Flying Cross, but drummed out for smoking marijuana. [The novel SACRIFICES is about this time.] Seeking to put youthful dreams behind, he resolved to get free and discover truth. After going from the DMZ to Woodstock in 1969, James tuned in, turned on, and dropped out. Three quick divorces. Sex, drugs, rock'n'roll, and religion. Psychedelics, Scientology, Wicca, Tao, and Jesus. Folk music composer, actor, singer, playwright, TV show host, occult publisher's editorial assistant, and founder of The Scribes Of Osiris. [The novel LOST ILLUSIONS is about this time.] Resolving to select a workable truth and settle down, in 1980 he returned to his home town Las Cruces, and worked various jobs raising daughter Nieve (politics and finance) and son Nathan (art and music). James now lives in Las Vegas, where he enjoys writing the bi-monthly newspaper column in which these articles first appeared, and is writing another novel, MERLINSPAWN, about being a dope runner pilot, and sports book bet runner.